T0289459

FISCAL RULES
AND ECONOMIC
SIZE IN LATIN
AMERICA AND
THE CARIBBEAN

FISCAL RULES AND ECONOMIC SIZE IN LATIN AMERICA AND THE CARIBBEAN

Fernando Blanco, Pablo Saavedra,
Friederike Koehler-Geib, and Emilia Skrok

 **WORLD BANK GROUP**

© 2020 International Bank for Reconstruction and Development / The World Bank
1818 H Street NW, Washington, DC 20433
Telephone: 202-473-1000; Internet: www.worldbank.org

Some rights reserved

1 2 3 4 23 22 21 20

This work is a product of the staff of The World Bank with external contributions. The findings, interpretations, and conclusions expressed in this work do not necessarily reflect the views of The World Bank, its Board of Executive Directors, or the governments they represent. The World Bank does not guarantee the accuracy of the data included in this work. The boundaries, colors, denominations, and other information shown on any map in this work do not imply any judgment on the part of The World Bank concerning the legal status of any territory or the endorsement or acceptance of such boundaries.

Nothing herein shall constitute or be considered to be a limitation upon or waiver of the privileges and immunities of The World Bank, all of which are specifically reserved.

RIGHTS AND PERMISSIONS

This work is available under the Creative Commons Attribution 3.0 IGO license (CC BY 3.0 IGO) http://creativecommons.org/licenses/by/3.0/igo. Under the Creative Commons Attribution license, you are free to copy, distribute, transmit, and adapt this work, including for commercial purposes, under the following conditions:

- **Attribution**—Please cite the work as follows: Blanco, Fernando, Pablo Saavedra, Friederike Koehler-Geib, and Emilia Skrok. 2020. *Fiscal Rules and Economic Size in Latin America and the Caribbean.* Latin American Development Forum. Washington, DC: World Bank. doi:10.1596/978-1-4648-1382-5. License: Creative Commons Attribution CC BY 3.0 IGO

- **Translations**—If you create a translation of this work, please add the following disclaimer along with the attribution: *This translation was not created by The World Bank and should not be considered an official World Bank translation. The World Bank shall not be liable for any content or error in this translation.*

- **Adaptations**—If you create an adaptation of this work, please add the following disclaimer along with the attribution: *This is an adaptation of an original work by The World Bank. Views and opinions expressed in the adaptation are the sole responsibility of the author or authors of the adaptation and are not endorsed by The World Bank.*

- **Third-party content**—The World Bank does not necessarily own each component of the content contained within the work. The World Bank therefore does not warrant that the use of any third-party-owned individual component or part contained in the work will not infringe on the rights of those third parties. The risk of claims resulting from such infringement rests solely with you. If you wish to re-use a component of the work, it is your responsibility to determine whether permission is needed for that re-use and to obtain permission from the copyright owner. Examples of components can include, but are not limited to, tables, figures, or images.

All queries on rights and licenses should be addressed to World Bank Publications, The World Bank Group, 1818 H Street NW, Washington, DC 20433, USA; e-mail: pubrights@worldbank.org.

ISBN (print): 978-1-4648-1382-5
ISBN (electronic): 978-1-4648-1581-2
DOI: 10.1596/978-1-4648-1382-5

Cover art and design: Bill Pragluski, Critical Stages, LLC.
Library of Congress Control Number: 2020944303.

Latin American Development Forum Series

This series was created in 2003 to promote debate, disseminate information and analysis, and convey the excitement and complexity of the most topical issues in economic and social development in Latin America and the Caribbean. It is sponsored by the Inter-American Development Bank, the United Nations Economic Commission for Latin America and the Caribbean, and the World Bank, and represents the highest quality in each institution's research and activity output. Titles in the series have been selected for their relevance to the academic community, policy makers, researchers, and interested readers, and have been subjected to rigorous anonymous peer review prior to publication.

Advisory Committee Members

Alicia Bárcena Ibarra, Executive Secretary, Economic Commission for Latin America and the Caribbean, United Nations

Inés Bustillo, Director, Washington Office, Economic Commission for Latin America and the Caribbean, United Nations

Eric Parrado Herrera, Chief Economist and General Manager, Research Department, Inter-American Development Bank

Elena Ianchovichina, Deputy Chief Economist of the Latin America and the Caribbean Region, World Bank

Martin Rama, Chief Economist of the Latin America and the Caribbean Region, World Bank

Roberto Rigobon, Professor of Applied Economics, Sloan School of Management, Massachusetts Institute of Technology

Ernesto Talvi, Director, Brookings Global-CERES Economic and Social Policy in Latin America Initiative

Andrés Velasco, CIEPLAN (Corporación de Estudios para Latinoamérica), Chile

Titles in the Latin American Development Forum Series

Does What You Export Matter? In Search of Empirical Guidance for Industrial Policies (2012) by Daniel Lederman and William F. Maloney

From Right to Reality: Incentives, Labor Markets, and the Challenge of Achieving Universal Social Protection in Latin America and the Caribbean (2012) by Helena Ribe, David Robalino, and Ian Walker

Breeding Latin American Tigers: Operational Principles for Rehabilitating Industrial Policies (2011) by Robert Devlin and Graciela Moguillansky

New Policies for Mandatory Defined Contribution Pensions: Industrial Organization Models and Investment Products (2010) by Gregorio Impavido, Esperanza Lasagabaster, and Manuel García-Huitrón

The Quality of Life in Latin American Cities: Markets and Perception (2010) by Eduardo Lora, Andrew Powell, Bernard M. S. van Praag, and Pablo Sanguinetti, editors

Discrimination in Latin America: An Economic Perspective (2010) by Hugo Ñopo, Alberto Chong, and Andrea Moro, editors

The Promise of Early Childhood Development in Latin America and the Caribbean (2010) by Emiliana Vegas and Lucrecia Santibáñez

Job Creation in Latin America and the Caribbean: Trends and Policy Challenges (2009) by Carmen Pagés, Gaëlle Pierre, and Stefano Scarpetta

China's and India's Challenge to Latin America: Opportunity or Threat? (2009) by Daniel Lederman, Marcelo Olarreaga, and Guillermo E. Perry, editors

Does the Investment Climate Matter? Microeconomic Foundations of Growth in Latin America (2009) by Pablo Fajnzylber, Jose Luis Guasch, and J. Humberto López, editors

Measuring Inequality of Opportunities in Latin America and the Caribbean (2009) by Ricardo Paes de Barros, Francisco H. G. Ferreira, José R. Molinas Vega, and Jaime Saavedra Chanduvi

The Impact of Private Sector Participation in Infrastructure: Lights, Shadows, and the Road Ahead (2008) by Luis Andres, Jose Luis

Remittances and Development: Lessons from Latin America (2008) by Pablo Fajnzylber and J. Humberto López, editors

Fiscal Policy, Stabilization, and Growth: Prudence or Abstinence? (2007) by Guillermo Perry, Luis Servén, and Rodrigo Suescún, editors

Raising Student Learning in Latin America: Challenges for the 21st Century (2007) by Emiliana Vegas and Jenny Petrow

Investor Protection and Corporate Governance: Firm-Level Evidence across Latin America (2007) by Alberto Chong and Florencio López-de-Silanes, editors

Natural Resources: Neither Curse nor Destiny (2007) by Daniel Lederman and William F. Maloney, editors

The State of State Reform in Latin America (2006) by Eduardo Lora, editor

Emerging Capital Markets and Globalization: The Latin American Experience (2006) by Augusto de la Torre and Sergio L. Schmukler

Beyond Survival: Protecting Households from Health Shocks in Latin America (2006) by Cristian C. Baeza and Truman G. Packard

Beyond Reforms: Structural Dynamics and Macroeconomic Vulnerability (2005) by José Antonio Ocampo, editor

Privatization in Latin America: Myths and Reality (2005) by Alberto Chong and Florencio López-de-Silanes, editors

Keeping the Promise of Social Security in Latin America (2004) by Indermit S. Gill, Truman G. Packard, and Juan Yermo

Lessons from NAFTA for Latin America and the Caribbean (2004) by Daniel Lederman, William F. Maloney, and Luis Servén

The Limits of Stabilization: Infrastructure, Public Deficits, and Growth in Latin America (2003) by William Easterly and Luis Servén, editors

Globalization and Development: A Latin American and Caribbean Perspective (2003) by José Antonio Ocampo and Juan Martin, editors

Is Geography Destiny? Lessons from Latin America (2003) by John Luke Gallup, Alejandro Gaviria, and Eduardo Lora Guasch, Thomas Haven, and Vivien Foster

All books in the Latin American Development Forum series are available for free at https://openknowledge.worldbank.org/handle/10986/2167.

Contents

Tables

Preface

This study and its background papers were prepared before the COVID-19 health pandemic engulfed the world, causing major economic fallout. The research and writing were conducted between 2017 and 2019. Part of the motivation for this work came from the authors' reflections following the collapse of commodity prices and ensuing terms-of-trade shock in 2014–15, which pulled many countries in Latin America and the Caribbean (LAC) into a recession and exposed massive fiscal and structural vulnerabilities. Only some countries had saved the commodities' windfall over 2010–14, including through the use of fiscal rules, creating the buffers needed to cushion this adverse shock. Like then, many LAC countries entered 2020 with limited fiscal buffers—at a time when the COVID-19 crisis requires a significant fiscal impulse to support jobs, firms, and households.

A lesson then and now is that fiscal policy mechanisms that enable countries to save in good times so that the savings can be used during rainy days—or stormy ones like those the world is enduring today—are critical. A well-designed, well-implemented fiscal rules framework can be essential in achieving this aim.

COVID-19's economic impact in the LAC region will be deep. According to the World Bank's *Global Economic Prospects* (June 2020), the LAC region's gross domestic product is expected to contract by more than 7 percent in 2020, leading to massive job losses and wiping out a large share of the poverty reduction achieved over the past two decades. Small countries in the region are being especially hard-hit given their low economic diversification and high exposure to external shocks. The output collapse of 2020 in this region is expected to outstrip the decline experienced during the Great Depression (1929–1933). In this context, fiscal policy has a big role to play, supporting aggregate demand and keeping a shock that could be temporary from dragging on longer. But as shown in this study and others, fiscal policy in the LAC region has tended to be highly procyclical, fueling ongoing economic upswings through public spending and worsening downswings through contractionary fiscal policy. When the COVID-19 crisis hit, the LAC region and most emerging economies were in a period of growing public spending, high public debt (compared with 2009 and 2014), and limited fiscal space overall to react countercyclically. Heightened global risk aversion will tighten access to credit markets, especially for highly indebted countries with more vulnerable macroeconomic positions.

So why is it critical to talk about fiscal rules today? Only the countries that saved during the good years, including through fiscal rule mechanisms, have and are employing their saved fiscal firepower to smooth the shock and protect their real economies and households. Indeed, establishing a fiscal rules framework today would not help in this crisis. These frameworks require careful design, a political consensus, and time to be implemented adequately, if they are to be ready and functioning by the next economic cycle. Thus, policy makers need to start thinking today about the need to improve fiscal frameworks and adopt fiscal rules. The COVID-19 crisis has shown us that "black swan" or tail-risk events might be more frequent than in the past. Aside from all of the good reasons for establishing a well-designed, well-implemented system of fiscal rules, which are detailed in this study, this ongoing global crisis has given policy makers another powerful reason for placing this policy on the front burner to rebuild the fiscal and institutional frameworks of LAC's and all emerging economies in a better and stronger way.

Carlos Felipe Jaramillo
Vice President
Latin America and the Caribbean Region
World Bank

Acknowledgments

This study is part of the Regional Studies Program of the Office of the Regional Chief Economist, Latin America and the Caribbean Vice Presidency of the World Bank. This main study was written by Fernando Blanco, Friederike Koehler-Geib, Pablo Saavedra, and Emilia Skrok.

The study was based on a series of background and research papers prepared by Alvaro Aguirre, Jan Gaska, Klaus Schmidt Hebbel, Viktoriya Hnatkovska, Paulina Ewa Holda, Friederike Koehler-Geib, Arthur Mendes, Steven Pennings, Emilia Skrok, and Raimundo Soto. Substantive contributions were provided by Vincent De Paul Tsoungui Belinga, James Sampi Bravo, Edgardo Favaro, Aleksandra Ignaczak, and Ana Maria Jul. Editorial and production assistance was provided by Elizabeth Forsythe, Amy Lynn Grossman, Alfred Imhoff, Patricia Katyama, and Sean Lothrop. Patricia Chacon Holt, Giselle Velasquez, and Miriam Villarroel provided excellent assistance.

The team would like to thank Jorge Thompson Araujo, Elena Ianchovichina, Daniel Lederman, Augusto de la Torre, and Carlos Vegh for their excellent advice and support. The team is also thankful to Jorge Thompson Araujo, César Calderón, Francisco Galrao Carneiro, Norbert Fiess, Zafer Mustafaoglu, and the anonymous peer reviewers from the Latin American Development Forum for their valuable comments.

About the Authors

Fernando Blanco is an economist who has specialized in macroeconomics and fiscal policy. He joined the World Bank in 2002 and has worked in the Africa, Latin America and the Caribbean, Middle East and North Africa, and South Asia regions in the Macroeconomics, Trade, and Investment Global Practice. Currently, he is the principal economist for Europe and Central Asia at the International Finance Corporation in the World Bank Group. Before joining the World Bank, he served as an associate researcher for the Institute of Applied Economics Research, at a government think tank in Brazil, and as a professor of public economics and international economics at the Brazilian Institute of Capital Markets and the Pontifical Catholic University of Rio de Janeiro. He holds a PhD in economics from the Pontifical Catholic University of Rio de Janeiro.

Friederike (Fritzi) Koehler-Geib is KfW Group's chief economist and head of Research. In this capacity, she analyzes with her team economic developments and growth trends in Germany, Europe, and the world. She has a particular focus on small and medium enterprises, the role of innovation and digitalization in improving productivity, as well as issues related to the goal of a climate-neutral economy. Previously, she spent more than 10 years at the World Bank, most recently as lead economist and program leader for Central America. She has published research and worked with policy makers in various countries on reforms regarding economic growth, financial crises, and fiscal policy with a focus on public expenditures and fiscal rules. She holds a PhD in economics from Ludwig Maximilian University of Munich and two master's degrees from University of St. Gallen, HEC Paris, and the University of Michigan.

Pablo Saavedra is an economist who has served in several positions of responsibility in various regions and departments at the World Bank. He is currently the World Bank's country director for Mexico. Previously, he served as manager of the World Bank's Macroeconomics and Fiscal Management Department for Latin America and the Caribbean, an economic adviser for the Policy and Strategy Department, a sector leader for Economic Policy, and senior economist for Belarus, Poland, and Ukraine, among other countries. He has conducted research and worked with policy makers in countries around the world to implement reforms on issues related to economic growth, including macroeconomics and fiscal policies, tax and spending policies, and fiscal rules. He holds a PhD from the Georgia Institute of Technology.

Emilia Skrok is a program leader in the World Bank's Macroeconomics, Fiscal Management, Governance, Poverty, and Equity Department. She joined the World Bank in 2005. Previously, she served as an economist on the Economic and Market Research Team at the Treasury Department of Bank PEKAO S.A., the largest private bank in Poland, and as a senior economist in the Department of Financial Policy, Analysis, and Statistics in Poland's Ministry of Finance. She has taught international comparative economics at the Warsaw School of Economics. Her research focuses on fiscal policy analysis, including tax and spending policies and fiscal institutions at both the national and subnational levels. She holds a PhD in economics from the SGH Warsaw School of Economics.

Abbreviations

EECU	Eastern Caribbean Currency Union
FDI	foreign direct investment
FRSI	Fiscal Rule Strength Index
GDP	gross domestic product
GNI	gross national income
LAC	Latin America and the Caribbean

Overview

Setting the Scene

The fiscal position of most countries in Latin America and the Caribbean (LAC) has deteriorated in the last decade. To address the flagging growth of gross domestic product (GDP) in the aftermath of the 2008 global financial crisis, governments across the region launched protracted expansions of spending, which in many cases eroded the fiscal buffers built in the precrisis period. Even though economic growth recovered as a result of massive terms-of-trade gains over 2010–14, governments did not use the economic upturn as an opportunity to improve their fiscal balances and curb indebtedness. On the contrary, government spending and fiscal deficits continued to grow (De la Torre, Ize, and Pienknagura 2015). Then, the commodity price shock in 2014–15 hampered GDP growth at a time when only a few countries had sufficient fiscal space to attenuate its negative effects; deficits and indebtedness deteriorated further. The LAC region's average fiscal deficit rose from 1.9 percent of GDP in 2000–08 to 3.5 percent in 2009–19, pushing the average stock of public debt from 41 percent of GDP in 2008 to 62 percent in 2019) (figure O.1).

Smaller countries in LAC have had markedly large fiscal deficits.[1] Between 2000 and 2019, these countries had an average fiscal deficit of 2.7 percent of GDP, far above the average of 0.5 percent for smaller countries worldwide and 2.2 percent for larger countries in the LAC region. The region's very small countries performed even worse, registering an average fiscal deficit of 3.2 percent of GDP versus a global average for very small countries of 0.1 percent. The average fiscal deficit for large economies in LAC was only marginally worse than the average for large countries worldwide, which suggests that the fiscal performance of smaller LAC countries is not associated solely with regional patterns; it is also associated with other features that are assessed in this study (figure O.2).

Due to large fiscal deficits, public debt levels have risen rapidly among small economies in LAC. By 2019, small LAC economies had an average debt stock of 66 percent of GDP, with an average of 76 percent for very small countries. Worldwide, small countries had a debt stock of 58 percent of GDP, with an average of 60 percent

1

Average Fiscal Balance and Debt Level as a Percentage of GDP in LAC Countries, 2000–08 versus 2009–19

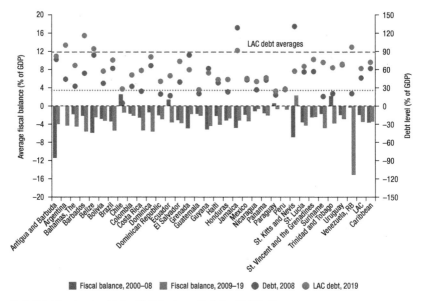

Source: Calculations based on data from World Development Indicators (World Bank).

for very small countries. In contrast, in LAC the average debt stock for larger countries was 42 percent of GDP, a level much lower than the worldwide average, where larger countries had an average debt level of 57 percent of GDP. Therefore, smaller countries in LAC, particularly the very small ones, exhibited higher indebtedness that cannot be attributed solely to their geographic location.

The poorer fiscal performance of smaller LAC countries is associated with their greater exposure to exogenous volatility, including natural disasters. Exogeneous factors have contributed to worsening fiscal balances and accelerating indebtedness in smaller countries in the region. Frequent, intense natural disasters have pressured government spending and negatively affected economic activity and government revenues. The negative impacts of frequent natural disasters suffered by small and very small LAC countries—particularly Caribbean countries—have resulted in significant slowdowns in GDP, high fiscal costs to repair damaged infrastructure, and high volatility of output and consumption when compared with large countries in the region (table O.1). In addition, due to their greater openness and lack of diversification, small economies are more vulnerable to terms-of-trade shocks, which have exacerbated the volatility of their fiscal revenues.

FIGURE O.2: Fiscal Balance as a Share of GDP in LAC and the World, by Country Size, 2000–17

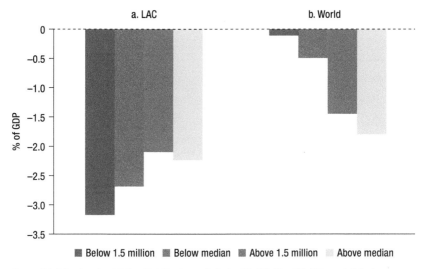

Sources: Calculations based on data from World Development Indicators (World Bank) and World Economic Outlook (International Monetary Fund).

FIGURE O.3: Government Debt as a Share of GDP in LAC and the World, by Country Size, 2017

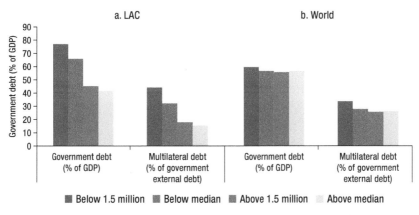

Sources: Calculations based on data from World Development Indicators (World Bank) and World Economic Outlook (International Monetary Fund).

TABLE O.1: Regression Coefficients of Government Spending Growth on GDP Growth in LAC and the World, by Country Size, 2000–15

Indicator	Large (above median)	Small (below median)	Very small (below 1.5 million)
LAC			
Total spending	0.65	0.72	1.94
Current spending	0.35	1.5	1.27
Government wage bill	0.20	0.96	—
Investment	2.30	2.51	3.45
World			
Government spending	0.59	0.74	0.84
Current spending	0.51	0.70	0.69
Government wage bill	0.40	0.78	0.80
Investment	1.10	1.73	1.69

Sources: Calculations based on data from World Development Indicators (World Bank) and World Economic Outlook (International Monetary Fund).
Note: — = not available.

At the same time, unsustainable, procyclical fiscal policies have intensified macroeconomic volatility in smaller LAC countries. Fiscal frameworks in many LAC countries have been unable to promote fiscal discipline or incentivize savings in good economic times to be used when negative shocks occur. Small countries in LAC have also exhibited strong procyclicality in government spending. Overspending in good years has left no room for countercyclical responses in downturns. Evidence presented in this study reveals that government spending and its components are considerably more procyclical in smaller countries, especially in very small ones. Moreover, very small countries in the LAC region exhibit a much higher degree of expenditure procyclicality than larger countries in the region and other very small countries worldwide. In small LAC countries, given the larger size of governments that is reflected in high ratios of government spending to GDP, the strong procyclicality of government spending results in extreme macroeconomic volatility.

High deficits, high indebtedness, and procyclical spending have exacerbated macroeconomic volatility in LAC's smaller countries and hampered their GDP growth. The strong volatility of international markets and the impact of the 2008 global financial crisis have disproportionately affected small economies, and high government deficits and debt have lowered their GDP growth rates even further. Between 2000 and 2017, the growth of GDP per capita among large countries worldwide averaged 4 percent per year,

FIGURE O.4: Growth and Volatility of GDP per Capita and Private Consumption in LAC and the World, by Country Size, 2000–17

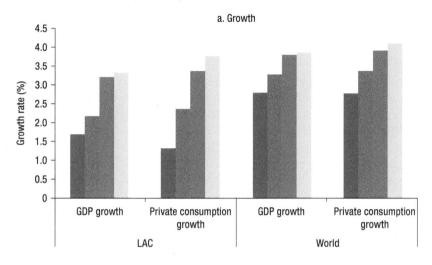

a. Growth

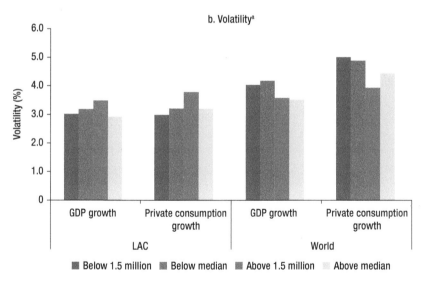

b. Volatility[a]

▇ Below 1.5 million   ▇ Below median   ▇ Above 1.5 million   ▨ Above median

Sources: Calculations based on data from World Development Indicators (World Bank) and World Economic Outlook (International Monetary Fund).
a. Volatility is measured as the standard deviation of the growth rate of each variable, expressed as a percentage.

compared with an average of 3.5 percent and 3.2 percent for small and very small economies, respectively (figure O.4). This pattern was even more pronounced in small LAC countries. Economic growth among small and very small economies was 20 and 34 percent lower, respectively, than growth in large countries in the LAC region, where growth was much lower than in the rest of the world.

High deficits and debt levels, together with heightened macroeconomic volatility have generated renewed interest in the use of fiscal rules as instruments that—if designed, established, and implemented adequately—can help, strengthening debt sustainability and smoothing output volatility over economic cycles. Following the recent global financial crisis, many countries worldwide strengthened their fiscal frameworks and improved the design of their fiscal rules. The adoption of medium-term fiscal frameworks, better budgeting and accounting practices, and more forceful enforcement and correction mechanisms, as well as the establishment of fiscal councils, and sovereign wealth funds are among the measures that have improved the institutional framework and the operation of fiscal rules. In addition, a new generation of fiscal rules has helped countries to design more flexible frameworks to attenuate the effects of adverse shocks, reduce cyclical fluctuations in output, or smooth the effect of commodity price volatility. Structural balance rules—combined fiscal rules, the integration of fiscal rules and sovereign wealth funds, and improved escape clauses—have been adopted to reduce the procyclicality of fiscal policy and preserve flexibility to accommodate fluctuations in the business cycle, severe economic slowdowns, and the impact of natural disasters.

Likewise, fiscal rules have become an important tool for enhancing the credibility of a country's macroeconomic management because they favor the transparency and predictability of fiscal policy. By establishing quantitative limits on fiscal balances, debt levels, expenditure growth, and other key fiscal aggregates, fiscal rules limit discretion and may insulate fiscal management from political pressure. Furthermore, fiscal rules may critically favor the transparency and predictability of fiscal policy and therefore enhance policy credibility. In turn, greater transparency and predictability facilitate access to capital markets, especially including during downturns.

Fiscal rules have also become part of a broader risk management strategy that encompasses the use of different instruments to attenuate volatility in countries facing more frequent and intense exogenous shocks. Risk transfer mechanisms shift the burden and costs of adverse shocks to another party. They include weather-related insurance to cope with natural disasters and other environmental hazards that negatively affect GDP growth as well as commodity price–related insurance or derivative instruments to protect government budgets from commodity price fluctuations. Precautionary or self-insurance instruments aim at building up buffers that help to mitigate the impact of negative shocks, including fiscal rules, stabilization and natural disaster funds, and contingent credit instruments that are used to finance expenditures triggered by adverse shocks.[2]

The benefits of adopting integrated risk management strategies and, in particular, fiscal rules appear to be greater in small economies in LAC. Smaller economies are more exposed to exogenous volatility, which is reflected in more frequent and intense natural disasters and in terms-of-trade shocks that have a bigger impact given their size. For this reason, smaller economies may obtain more benefits from the use of risk transfer mechanisms and self-insurance instruments. In particular, using more sustainable, more output-stabilizing, and less procyclical fiscal policy in more volatile economic contexts tends to reap more benefits. In addition, enhanced predictability and credibility of fiscal policy are useful in turbulent periods because greater predictability may facilitate access to financial markets and thus mitigate the impact of adverse shocks.

Fiscal Rules and Economic Size

This study seeks to make analytical and practical contributions to the design and implementation of fiscal rules in smaller countries. The effectiveness of fiscal rules in achieving fiscal sustainability and stabilizing output depends on the specific features of the business cycles in each country. It also depends on the type of shocks and the magnitude of shocks to be smoothed, which can be related to the size of the economy. The study also reviews the performance of fiscal rules worldwide and provides information on which types of rules are used the most, which have the best record of compliance, which are the most effective in promoting debt sustainability and preventing procyclical fiscal policies, and which tend to improve their performance. This study provides practical policy directions drawn from international experience to assist policy makers in designing and implementing more effective fiscal rules.

The relationship between fiscal rules and economic size has not been examined in detail in the literature. Policy makers must select the fiscal rule or set of rules best suited to the features of their country's business cycle, exchange rate regime, type of shocks faced, and macroeconomic characteristics, among others. Smaller countries, for example, tend to have more volatile business cycles and face more frequent shocks, such as natural disasters and terms-of-trade downswings. Moreover, business cycles in smaller economies appear to be especially asymmetric, their fiscal revenues tend to be more volatile, and their fiscal policies are generally more procyclical than those of larger countries. These particularities can affect how fiscal rules function and are important for determining the type of rules selected and their technical design.

Policy makers also need to consider the institutional and technical capabilities required for implementing different types of fiscal rules. This study highlights the role of initial conditions in determining the effectiveness of fiscal rules. In particular, initial conditions refer to the institutional framework surrounding fiscal policy and the technical capacities of governments which are decisive factors influencing the functioning and performance of fiscal rules. Both conventional wisdom and a large body of literature suggest that countries with fiscal rules have better fiscal outcomes. Practical experience also suggests that fiscal rules work best when their design reflects the government's capacity constraints and its institutional and policy framework.[3]

This study evaluates not only the impact of the presence or absence of fiscal rules on fiscal policy objectives and outcomes but also how compliance with the provisions of the established rules affects the achievement of those objectives and which institutional factors affect compliance itself.

While the study focuses on smaller economies, its findings also have application to larger countries. The typical features of smaller economies and their business cycles are also present, albeit to a lesser degree, in larger economies. In fact, the numerical thresholds used in the literature to separate smaller from larger economies are arbitrary. The policy implications of economic size in the design of fiscal rules found in this study can be, and indeed are, valid in larger economies. Similarly, the findings of this study also have cross-region policy implications, as the sources of heightened volatility—greater openness, low diversification, and high exposure to natural disasters, among other features—are common to smaller countries worldwide, albeit to different extents.

This study is organized in four chapters and this overview. Chapter 1 describes the structural features of small economies, discussing how they influence the business cycle, particularly in the LAC region. Chapter 2 assesses the compliance with fiscal rules worldwide and identifies the institutional factors affecting compliance and the performance of different fiscal rules vis-à-vis their objectives. Chapter 3 provides analytical input for the choice and design of fiscal rules, taking into consideration the unique macroeconomic policy challenges faced by smaller economies. Chapter 4 summarizes the main findings of this study and outlines policy implications.

Small Countries: Structural Features, Business Cycles, and Recent Economic Performance

Throughout this study, a country's size is defined primarily by the size of its population. To identify the specific features of small countries, two approaches are taken. The first is a discrete approach that recognizes the heterogeneity within small economies. It defines "smaller" countries as having populations below the global median of 4.1 million and "very small" countries as having populations below 1.5 million.[4] The group of smaller countries refers to the 86 countries with populations below the global median of 4.1 million, while the group of very small countries refers to the 51 countries with populations below 1.5 million. The LAC region is home to 18 smaller countries, including 12 very small countries, or 24 percent of all very small countries worldwide.[5] The second approach is a continuous approach that assesses the effects of population on fiscal variables using a continuous measure of population across countries and over time, without stratification.

While heterogeneous in their level of development, most smaller countries share several key structural features:

- *High levels of trade openness.* Due to their smaller labor forces and domestic markets, which limit the formation of economies of scale and agglomeration, smaller economies tend to rely heavily on international trade.

- *Limited economic diversification.* Due to their factor endowments, smaller countries tend to specialize and focus on a narrow range of economic activities, leading to concentrated production and export structures.

- *Large governments (in relative terms).* Due to their inability to leverage economies of scale in public administration, smaller countries tend to face higher unit costs for public goods and services. This difficulty is particularly the case for "very small" economies that have a higher ratio of public spending to GDP.

- *Less flexible exchange rate regimes.* Due to their structural vulnerability to terms-of-trade shocks and the high fixed costs of operating a domestic monetary policy, smaller countries tend to adopt less flexible exchange rate regimes.

- *Vulnerability to natural disasters.* Due to their small geographic size, smaller countries tend to be more susceptible to natural disasters and climate change and to experience greater economic impacts from them than larger countries. This vulnerability is particularly acute in the smaller islands of the Caribbean, the Pacific Islands, and similar countries in other regions, which means that geographic location (such as island territories) is another factor explaining their high vulnerability to natural disasters.

Smaller countries experience greater fluctuations in GDP and other macroeconomic aggregates; moreover, exogenous shocks are exacerbated by the structural factors of these economies described above. Almost 45 percent of smaller LAC countries and 70 percent of very small LAC countries use fixed exchange rates. Fixed exchange rate regimes (figure O.5, panel a) prevent smaller economies from accommodating to terms-of-trade shocks, resulting in longer and deeper slowdowns. In the same way, external terms-of-trade shocks are magnified by their high trade openness (figure O.5, panel b), and their more concentrated production and export structures leave them more vulnerable to terms-of-trade shocks, also hampering swift recoveries (figure O.5, panel c).[6] Their relatively large public sectors increase the impact of procyclical fiscal policies on output, investment, and consumption.

Natural disasters in smaller LAC countries tend to be more frequent (higher probability of occurrence) and costly (more intense impacts). On average, hurricanes, tropical storms, volcanic eruptions, landslides, floods, and droughts in small LAC countries inflict losses that are roughly 400 percent higher than those inflicted on large states, while the losses experienced by very small LAC countries are 620 percent higher. More frequent and intense natural disasters also exacerbate the volatility of output growth, either by deepening economic downturns or abruptly interrupting economic upturns (figure O.6).

Volatility is also heightened by fiscal policy and, in particular, by procyclical spending in smaller countries. Government expenditures are more volatile in smaller countries than in larger countries. The correlation between expenditure volatility and economic size is seen both by comparing subsamples of small and large countries

FIGURE O.5: **Structural Features of Countries in LAC and the World, by Country Size**

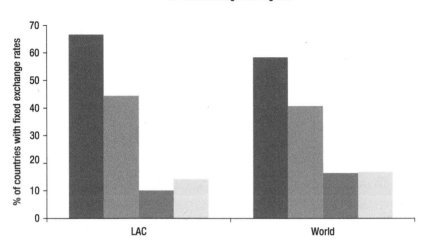

a. Fixed exchange rate regimes

b. Openness to trade

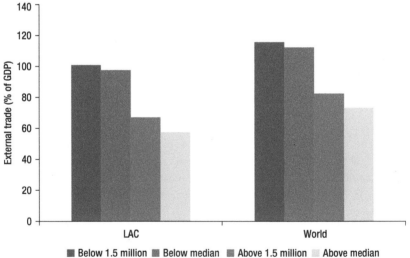

■ Below 1.5 million ■ Below median ■ Above 1.5 million ▨ Above median

(continued on next page)

FISCAL RULES AND ECONOMIC SIZE IN LATIN AMERICA AND THE CARIBBEAN

FIGURE O.5: **Structural Features of Countries in LAC and the World, by Country Size** *(continued)*

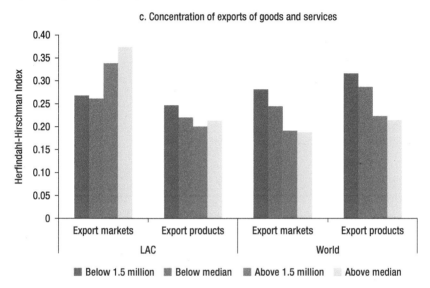

c. Concentration of exports of goods and services

Legend: ■ Below 1.5 million ■ Below median ■ Above 1.5 million ░ Above median

Sources: Calculations based on data from World Development Indicators (World Bank) and World Economic Outlook (International Monetary Fund).

and by conducting regression analysis. Government expenditures also appear to be more procyclical in smaller than in larger countries. Although this result is not statistically significant, stronger procyclicality is observed for all spending categories. Again, one of the structural features of small countries—in particular, their relatively large public sectors—magnifies the impact of procyclical fiscal policies on output, investment, and consumption.

Indeed, the evidence presented in this study confirms that smaller countries have a more volatile business cycle. GDP is more volatile in smaller economies than in larger countries, as evidenced by the negative relationship between population size and volatility shown in table O.2. Other macroeconomic variables are also more volatile in smaller countries. Indeed, fluctuations in private and government consumption, total and private investment, and external balances are more volatile in countries with smaller populations. These results are robust to the level of economic development (measured by per capita income) and other control variables (columns 2 and 3 in table O.2).[7]

In addition, business cycles are more asymmetric: cyclical contractions are deeper in smaller countries than in larger countries, while expansions are shorter. Contractions are more pronounced in smaller countries, with the average cumulative drop in GDP equal to 7 percent, as opposed to 5 percent in large countries. The average duration of expansions is shorter in small countries (at 17.6 quarters) relative to large

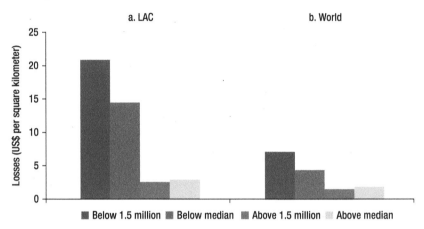

Sources: Calculations based on data from World Development Indicators (World Bank) and World Economic Outlook (International Monetary Fund).

countries (at 23.9 quarters). However, table O.3 also shows that the duration of contractions is similar in smaller and larger countries.[8]

A Snapshot of Fiscal Rules

Fiscal rules can enhance macroeconomic management by ensuring debt sustainability and favoring the stabilization of output fluctuations. These potential effects are even more critical in smaller countries. As described above, smaller countries tend to face more severe shocks and experience greater macroeconomic volatility. In addition, smaller countries have larger public sectors relative to their economic size. Therefore, public spending has a greater role to play in changes in aggregate demand. For this reason, if countries have more procyclical fiscal policies, this role can be particularly problematic, as fiscal policy is often the only stabilizing instrument available in many small countries. In this context, fiscal rules can be very useful in reinforcing the government's commitment to fiscal sustainability, attenuating fluctuations in the business cycle, creating a more predictable fiscal policy framework, and building buffers against adverse macroeconomic shocks when these rules are accompanied by sovereign wealth funds such as savings or stabilization funds.

TABLE O.2: **Regression of Volatilities on Continuous Population Size (in Population)**

Indicator	Baseline (1)	Controlling by economic development (2)	With all controls (3)
GDP	−0.06***	−0.06***	−0.10***
Gross national income	−0.17***	−0.17***	−0.16***
Private consumption	−0.08***	−0.09***	−0.06
Government consumption	−0.01	−0.03	−0.07*
Total investment	−0.06**	−0.06**	−0.08***
Private investment	−0.06	−0.05	−0.09
Government investment	−0.04	−0.04	0.11
Current account / GDP	−0.18***	−0.18***	−0.20***
Trade balance / GDP	−0.21***	−0.24***	−0.22***

Source: Hnatkovska and Koehler-Geib 2017.
*** $p < .01$ ** $p < .05$ * $< p .10$.

TABLE O.3: **Duration and Amplitude of Expansions and Contractions of GDP, by Country Size**

Indicator	Obs.	Duration (in quarters) Mean	Std. dev.	Amplitude Mean	Std. dev.
Small					
Expansions	22	17.62	10.0	0.29	0.21
Contractions	22	4.3	2.26	−0.07	0.06
Large					
Expansions	47	23.87	11.63	0.29	0.16
Contractions	46	4.38	2.71	−0.05	0.05

Source: Hnatkovska and Koehler-Geib 2017.
Note: Obs. = number of observations; std. dev. = standard deviation. Based on quarterly data for 69 countries (39 high-income and 30 low- and middle-income) from 1960 to 2015. Small is defined as countries with populations below 4.151 million. Large is defined as countries with populations above 4.151 million.

Fiscal rules are designed primarily to promote fiscal sustainability, although the stabilization of output fluctuations has become an increasingly important objective. The literature classifies fiscal rules according to the fiscal aggregate they target (figure O.7):

1. *Balance rules* establish targets for different categories of government fiscal balances (overall, primary, or current balances). According to the macrofiscal objectives they pursue, there are two types of balance rules:

a. *Budget balance rules* define numerical targets for actual government fiscal balances, normally in terms of GDP. Budget balance rules have direct, strong links with debt sustainability objectives because their numerical targets directly affect debt dynamics and are defined to ensure that the debt-to-GDP ratio converges with a targeted debt level. Without added features, they tend to foster procyclical fiscal policies, thus exacerbating economic fluctuations.

b. *Structural balance rules* target the estimated budget balance that would result if output were at its long-term potential; they filter out one-time fiscal transactions that do not affect the intertemporal fiscal position of the government (for example, privatizations, extraordinary spending related to policy changes such as social security reforms and civil service reforms). In countries where commodity export proceeds are relevant, this type of rule takes into account the effect of commodity price cycles on fiscal balances. Different from budget balance rules, structural balance rules focus mainly on stabilizing economic fluctuations to prevent procyclical fiscal stances, with debt sustainability as a more subdued objective.[9]

2. *Debt rules* set numerical limits for public debt, typically as a percentage of GDP. Because of their explicit link to debt expressed as stocks or ratios, debt rules tend to be the most direct tool for ensuring that fiscal policy is consistent with sustainable debt levels. Without added design features, debt rules alone tend to promote procyclical fiscal policies that exacerbate economic cycles, especially when actual debt levels are close to the ceiling and the space for output smoothing is restricted. When actual debt levels

FIGURE O.7: **A Basic Taxonomy of Fiscal Rules**

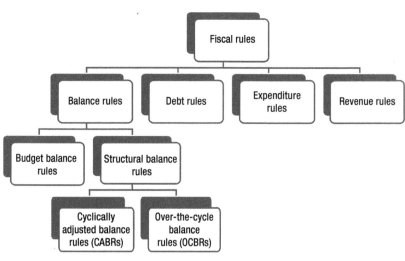

Source: World Bank.

are far from the targets, debt rules do not provide clear guidance for the definition of annual budget targets.

3. *Expenditure rules* establish limits on the growth of government spending. One of their key functions is to contain the size of government. As they establish fixed targets for the growth of government expenditures, expenditure rules also reduce spending procyclicality and support output stabilization. However, by themselves, they are less effective than either budget balance or debt rules in ensuring debt sustainability, especially during downturns.

4. *Revenue rules* set floors or ceilings on government revenue. They can help to improve revenue collection or prevent an excessive tax burden. Revenue rules do not ensure debt sustainability. In addition, revenue rules that set revenue floors or ceilings tend to introduce procyclicality because they prevent the operation of automatic stabilizers on the revenue side of the budget. Nonetheless, by defining the use of windfall or higher-than-expected revenues, some revenue rules can indirectly support debt sustainability and reduce procyclical and volatile spending.

Many countries adopt a combination of fiscal rules, either to achieve multiple policy goals or to reinforce their effect on key fiscal aggregates. Combining budget balance or debt rules with expenditure rules helps to attain sustainable debt levels and output stabilization simultaneously by lessening spending procyclicality. The combination of debt rules with budget balance rules reinforces the impact on debt sustainability because debt ceilings only constrain government deficits when debt levels are close to the established ceiling. By limiting the growth of government spending, this combination provides operational guidance to fiscal policy even when actual debt is far from the targeted level.

Fiscal rules may also be complemented by sovereign wealth funds, such as stabilization and savings funds. These funds are commonly used for accumulating or managing natural resource revenues, extraordinary revenues (for example, privatization proceeds) or the overperformance of revenue collection related to a variety of reasons. Stabilization funds insulate the government budget from commodity price volatility by accumulating resources in periods of higher-than-historical or higher-than-average prices and disbursing funds to the budget at lower-than-historical or lower-than-average prices. Stabilization funds can also be implemented to attenuate fluctuations in government revenue associated with the business cycle. Given the exhaustible nature of natural resource revenues, savings funds can also set aside fiscal resources for longer-term objectives, such as preparing for the needs of an aging population or promoting intergenerational equity in the distribution of resource rents.

Integrating the operation of a sovereign wealth fund with fiscal rules is highly desirable. To make the fiscal framework coherent and effective, the criteria for accumulation and disbursement of sovereign wealth funds need to be consistent with the design and operation of fiscal rule(s). The proper integration of a sovereign wealth fund with the overall fiscal framework can be achieved by linking the accumulation of funds (flows to the fund) and disbursement (flows from the fund to the budget) to the targets defined in the fiscal rule. Indeed, the sovereign wealth fund balance should be a "mirror image" of the government's budget, structural balance, expenditure, and revenue rules. This linkage can also help to improve the transparency of the system.

Finally, the use of independent fiscal councils can reinforce the functioning of fiscal rules. Fiscal councils strengthen the commitment of fiscal authorities because they raise the reputational and political costs of deviations to the rule by monitoring compliance and sometimes by providing independent technical views on macrofiscal projections. Fiscal councils can also provide impartial assessments of the fiscal impact of policy decisions on medium-term fiscal sustainability, promoting awareness and public debate on fiscal policy choices. Having an independent fiscal council (or a high degree of autonomy on core functions) enhances the credibility of the overall institutional framework where fiscal rules operate.

Fiscal Rules in Practice: Presence, Compliance, and Effectiveness

Presence of Fiscal Rules

The adoption of fiscal rules to guide fiscal policy has become increasingly common worldwide among both larger and smaller countries (figure O.8). The number of countries adopting fiscal rules has increased steadily, rising from 7 in 1990 to 49 in 2000 and reaching 92 in 2015. Out of the 92 countries with fiscal rules, 48 are larger countries and 44 are smaller countries. Debt rules and balance rules are the most common, although the use of expenditure rules and a combination of rules is on the rise.[10] In 2015 more than 70 debt rules and balance rules were in place worldwide. Although they remain relatively scarce, the number of expenditure rules has increased sharply in recent years, rising from 23 in 2011 to 45 in 2015. In small countries, the number of expenditure rules tripled from 7 to 19 over the period. Many countries now combine a budget balance rule with a debt rule, a budget balance rule with an expenditure rule, or a debt rule with an expenditure rule.

The adoption of fiscal rules is also increasing in LAC, with the number of countries with rules rising from 6 (or 19 percent of LAC countries) in the 1990s to 17 (or 52 percent) in 2015; of these, 10 (out of 18) are smaller countries (figure O.9). Indeed, fiscal rules are as common in smaller LAC countries as they are in smaller countries in the rest of the world and in large LAC countries. The number of smaller LAC countries adopting fiscal rules rose significantly as a result of the adoption of supranational rules by the Eastern Caribbean Currency Union (ECCU), which encompasses six very small Caribbean countries.

Broadly, LAC countries also follow international trends in the types of rules that are commonly used, but smaller countries in the region are somewhat behind international patterns in the adoption of expenditure and combined rules. While debt rules are the most popular type of fiscal rule in the LAC region, LAC countries tend to use

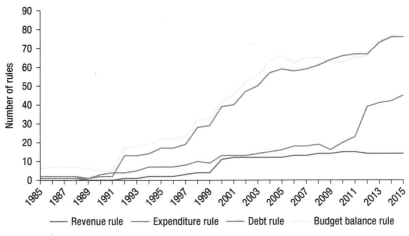

FIGURE O.8: **Number of Fiscal Rules, by Type of Rule, 1985–2015**

Source: Calculations based on data from the Fiscal Rules Dataset (IMF 2015).

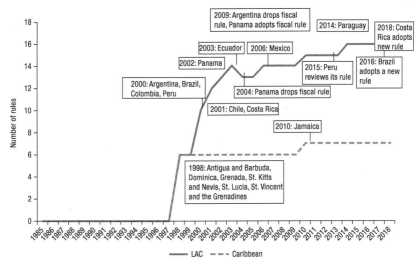

FIGURE O.9: **Number of National or Supranational Fiscal Rules in LAC, 1985–2019**

Source: Based on data from the Fiscal Rules Dataset (IMF 2015).

fewer debt rules and balance rules than countries in other regions; however, due to the ECCU's combined debt and balance rules, smaller (and very small countries) in LAC use more debt rules and balance rules than their larger regional peers. LAC countries have increasingly adopted expenditure rules, but small LAC countries only began adopting them in 2015. Furthermore, smaller countries and LAC countries are somewhat less likely to use combined rules than large countries and countries in other regions (figure O.10).

FIGURE O.10: Use of Fiscal Rules, by Type of Rule, Region, and Country Size, 2015

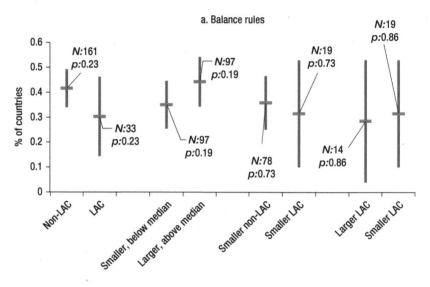

a. Balance rules

b. Debt rules

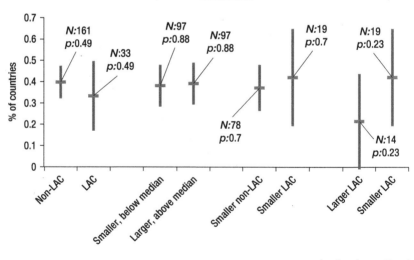

(continued on next page)

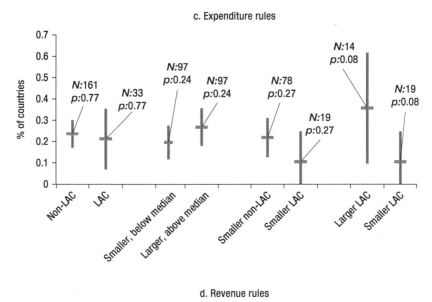

c. Expenditure rules

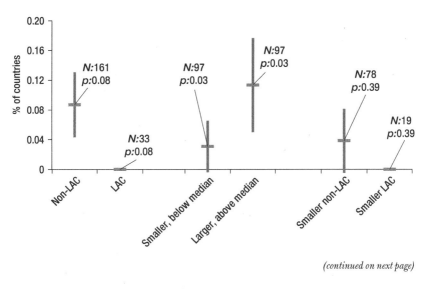

d. Revenue rules

(continued on next page)

FIGURE O.10: Use of Fiscal Rules, by Type of Rule, Region, and Country Size, 2015 (continued)

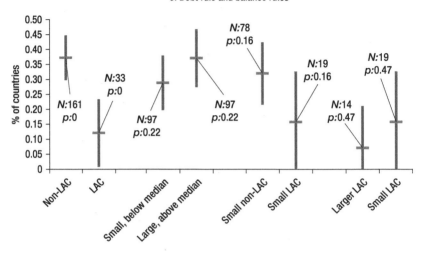

e. Debt rule and balance rules

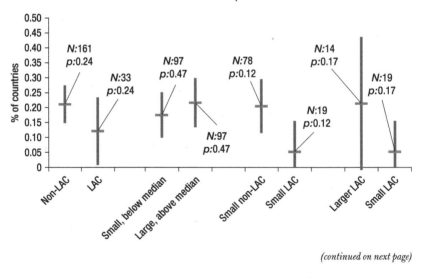

f. Debt rule and expenditure rules

(continued on next page)

g. Balance rule and expenditure rule

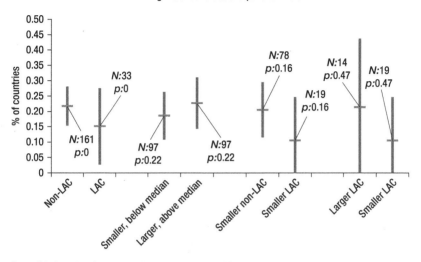

Source: Calculations based on data from the Fiscal Rules Dataset (IMF 2015).
Note: Figure shows the number of countries using each type of rule as a share of all countries in each region and size group. Vertical lines = 95 percent confidence interval for the sample average. Horizontal lines = sample averages. N = number of observations in each category. p = p-values for the test that the average of a given indicator for each subgroup is equal to the average outside the group. The figure makes four comparisons: (a) between non-LAC and LAC countries; (b) between smaller and larger countries; (c) between smaller non-LAC and LAC countries; and (d) between larger and smaller LAC countries.

Compliance with Fiscal Rules

The adoption of fiscal rules does not necessarily mean that they are respected. An analysis of compliance over 2000–15 conducted for this study reveals a significant gap between the presence of fiscal rules and actual compliance. Compliance reflects each government's ability and commitment to remain observing the statutory parameters established by the fiscal rule. Compliance varies from country to country, between periods, and by type of rule. Compliance rates fell drastically in the aftermath of the global financial crisis but have recovered somewhat in recent years. Debt rules had the highest compliance rates over the period.[11]

Smaller LAC countries have lower compliance than both larger LAC countries and smaller countries worldwide. This suggests that compliance cannot be associated directly with regional patterns. From lower levels in the early 2000s, average compliance rates among LAC countries were increasing in the period before the global financial crisis, becoming comparable to those of countries in other regions.

Nonetheless, while overall compliance rates in LAC have risen over time, compliance among smaller LAC countries has fallen. While compliance rates fell globally in the aftermath of the global financial crisis, the drop was especially deep in smaller LAC countries. In the same vein, compliance rates have recovered globally. This rebound has also occurred in larger LAC countries, which have recovered to their precrisis levels, but not in smaller LAC countries. Compliance in smaller LAC countries is lower than in smaller countries worldwide (figure O.11, panel a). Indeed, for the period 2000–15, although compliance rates in LAC and non-LAC countries and in smaller and larger countries worldwide were similar, compliance rates were much lower in smaller LAC countries than in the rest of the world (figure O.11, panel b).[12]

Compliance rates also differ by type of rule, with debt rules having the highest compliance rates over 2000–15, balance rules having the lowest, and compliance with expenditure rules increasing steadily since 2008. Expenditure rules now have the highest rates of compliance. Because debt rules apply to a stock variable (public debt) rather than to a flow, and a country can be far from its debt ceiling, the effects of fiscal expansions or contractions are weaker on debt than on fiscal balances, unless very strong macroeconomic shocks substantially increase the debt-to-GDP ratio. Thus debt rules tend to have higher compliance rates. By contrast, balance rules have the lowest compliance rates, as they establish a target on annual balances that are highly sensitive to contemporaneous macroeconomic shocks. Countries that apply structural balance rules or cyclically adjusted rules, which are better able to cope with growth shocks, have somewhat higher compliance rates. Compliance with expenditure rules has increased, and this type of rule has the highest compliance rate, as expenditure is the fiscal aggregate that fiscal authorities can control most directly (figure O.12).

Smaller countries in LAC have lower compliance rates regardless of the type of fiscal rule adopted. The LAC region has had better performance in complying with balance and debt rules than the rest of the world. A similar situation is observed for smaller countries worldwide, which have had higher compliance with both balance rules and debt rules than larger countries. While country size and geographic location do not seem to influence compliance rates by type of rule, smaller LAC countries have much lower compliance with both balance and debt rules, and they have not adopted expenditure rules so far.

Compliance is influenced by the fiscal framework surrounding the operation of fiscal rules. The fiscal framework encompasses a set of laws, regulations, institutions, and instruments that shape fiscal policies and support their implementation. A Fiscal Rule Strength Index (FRSI) was used to measure the institutional framework of fiscal rules.[13] The FRSI reflects five dimensions of rule strength: (1) statutory basis of the rule, (2) monitoring arrangements, (3) enforcement mechanisms, (4) coverage of the fiscal accounts to which the rule is applied, and (5) definition of escape clauses.

Results from this study confirm that a strong institutional and policy framework facilitates compliance with fiscal rules. Higher FRSI values are correlated with

FIGURE O.11: Compliance with Fiscal Rules, by Country Size and Region, 2000–15

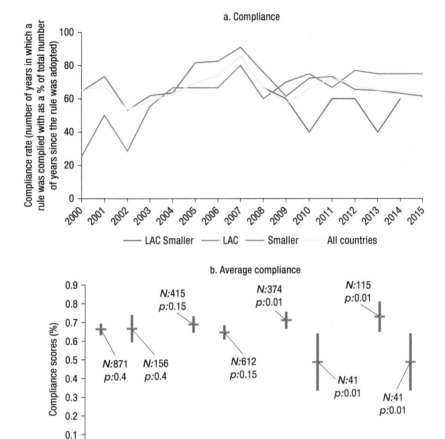

Sources: Calculations based on World Bank data on compliance with fiscal rules; Skrok et al. 2017.
Note: Panel a shows the number of countries complying with fiscal rules as a share of all countries in each region and size group. 1 = full compliance and 0 = noncompliance. Thus a score of 0.9 implies that a given country group complied with its fiscal rules in 90 percent of observations over the period. Vertical lines = 95 percent confidence interval for the sample average. Horizontal lines = sample averages. N = number of observations in each category. p = p-values for the test that the average of a given indicator for each subgroup is equal to the average outside the group. Smaller indicates countries with populations below 1.5 million. Panel b makes four comparisons: (a) between non-LAC and LAC countries; (b) between smaller and larger countries; (c) between smaller non-LAC and LAC countries; and (d) between larger and smaller LAC countries.

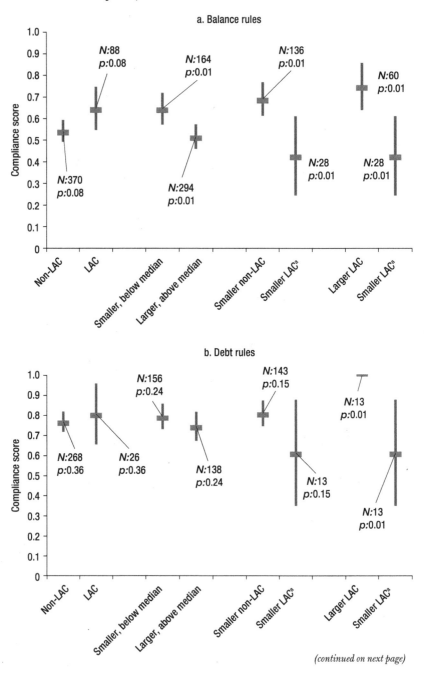

FIGURE O.12: Compliance with Fiscal Rules in LAC and the World, by Type of Rule and Country Size, 2000–15

a. Balance rules

b. Debt rules

(continued on next page)

c. Expenditure rules

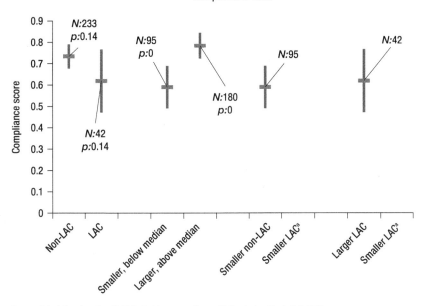

Sources: Calculations based on World Bank data on compliance with fiscal rules; Skrok et al. 2017.
Note: Figure shows the number of countries complying with each type of rule as a share of all countries in each region and size group. Vertical lines = 95 percent confidence interval for the sample average. Horizontal lines = sample averages. *N* = number of observations in each category. *p* = *p*-values for the test that the average of a given indicator for each subgroup is equal to the average outside the group. The figure makes four comparisons: (a) between non-LAC and LAC countries; (b) between smaller and larger countries; (c) between smaller non-LAC and LAC countries; and (d) between larger and smaller LAC countries.
a. No observations.

higher compliance rates (figure O.13). Individual dimensions have different effects on compliance, depending on the type of fiscal rule. In particular, the most important factors influencing compliance rates are the coverage of fiscal accounts to which the rule is applied and its enforcement mechanisms. The broader the coverage applied to balance rules and debt rules, the higher the compliance rate. Formal enforcement procedures—such as automatic correction mechanisms, predetermined consequences for noncompliance, and clearly defined authority to take corrective action—appear to increase compliance with balance rules. The legal basis of the rule and its monitoring arrangements appear to have little or no impact on compliance.

An interesting finding is that expenditure rules appear to require lower levels of institutional capacity, and this does not affect their compliance rates (figure O.13, panel a). Indeed, expenditure rules seem to be less demanding of technical and

FIGURE O.13: Fiscal Rule Strength Index (FSRI), by Type of Rule and Compliance, 1985–2013

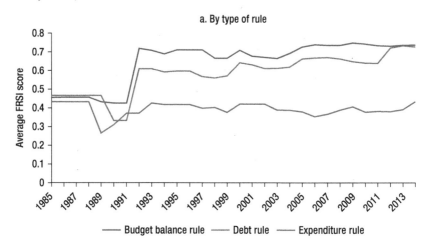

a. By type of rule

Budget balance rule ——— Debt rule ——— Expenditure rule

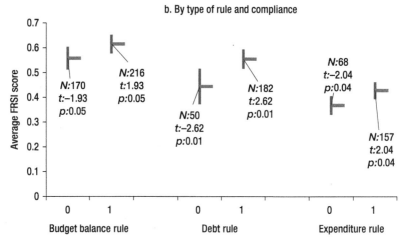

b. By type of rule and compliance

Sources: Calculations based on World Bank data on compliance with fiscal rules; Skrok et al. 2017.
Note: In panel b, 0 value = noncompliance and 1 = compliance. Vertical lines = 95 percent confidence interval for the sample average. Horizontal lines = sample averages. N = number of observations in each category. p = p-values for the test that the average of a given indicator for each subgroup is equal to the average outside the group. 0 = no compliance, 1 = compliance.

institutional capacity and require lower FRSI values than both budget balance and debt rules. At the individual level, regression results indicate that any of five dimensions of the FRSI has a significant impact on rates of compliance with expenditure rules. Therefore, expenditure rules are an attractive option in countries with weaker technical and institutional capacity to ensure high compliance rates.

Performance of Fiscal Rules

This study provides evidence that compliance strengthens the positive effects of the adoption of fiscal rules on fiscal outcomes. Cross-country analyses, centered mainly on high-income countries, have found that the *presence* of fiscal rules is associated with improved fiscal discipline (Debrun et al. 2008, 2013; European Commission 2009; Fall et al. 2015; Iara and Wolff 2011; Marneffe et al. 2011). These cross-country studies regard the *presence* of fiscal rules without accounting for the extent to which governments actually comply with them. The empirical assessment undertaken for this study differentiates presence from compliance, and its results suggest that the improvement of fiscal outcomes associated with the *presence* of fiscal rules is reinforced among countries that not only adopt rules but actually *comply* with them. Figure O.14, panel a, shows that compliance with balance rules improves debt sustainability as measured by the responsiveness of the primary balance to changes in the stock of debt, while both the presence of and compliance with debt rules have a positive, significant impact on fiscal sustainability.[14]

Results also show that fiscal rules generally appear to be more effective in large countries. Although actual compliance reinforces the positive impact on the responsiveness of the primary balance, in larger countries the presence of debt rules and expenditure rules already has a positive impact on the responsiveness of the primary balance to changes in debt. Among smaller countries, adopting fiscal rules has no statistically significant impact on debt sustainability, but complying with debt rules has a substantially positive impact on debt sustainability (figure O.14, panel b).

The findings of this study indicate that debt rules tend to have a greater impact on debt when they are accompanied by fiscal councils. Worldwide, balance rules, debt rules, and expenditure rules by themselves are not associated with lower debt levels unless institutional mechanisms such as fiscal councils are also in place. A debt rule combined with a fiscal council is associated with a reduction in public debt, as fiscal councils increase the probability of compliance. Moreover, countries that comply with balance rules have lower debt levels, but this relationship does not hold among LAC countries. Expenditure rules are associated with lower debt levels in LAC (figure O.15, panel a).

Similarly, the presence of any type of fiscal rule has a positive but statistically insignificant effect on fiscal balances, but when rules are actually observed or are accompanied by a sovereign wealth fund, their positive effects are strengthened. Worldwide, the presence of budget balance rules improves fiscal balances, but this positive effect is not statistically significant. It becomes significant in countries that comply with balance rules. Sovereign wealth funds have a positive, significant effect on fiscal balances. Globally, budget balance rules have the expected positive results on improving the fiscal balance. Yet the opposite result is found for Latin American countries. One possible explanation is that LAC countries had initially imposed high fiscal surpluses targets that were replaced by the establishment of fiscal rules that defined lower albeit more permanent targets. An alternative, but related, explanation is that

FIGURE O.14: **Impact of Fiscal Rules on the Responsiveness of the Primary Balance to Changes in the Stock of Debt, by Type of Rule and Country Size**

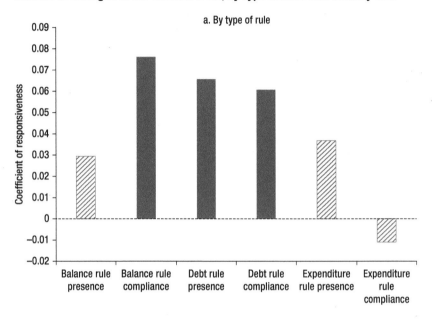

a. By type of rule

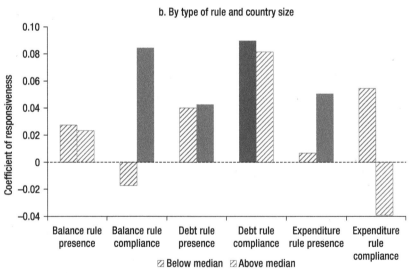

b. By type of rule and country size

⊠ Below median ⊠ Above median

Sources: Calculations based on World Bank data on compliance with fiscal rules; Skrok et al. 2017.
Note: A positive coefficient indicates that the fiscal rule strengthens the responsiveness of the primary balance to an increase in the debt stock. The solid fill denotes statistical significance.

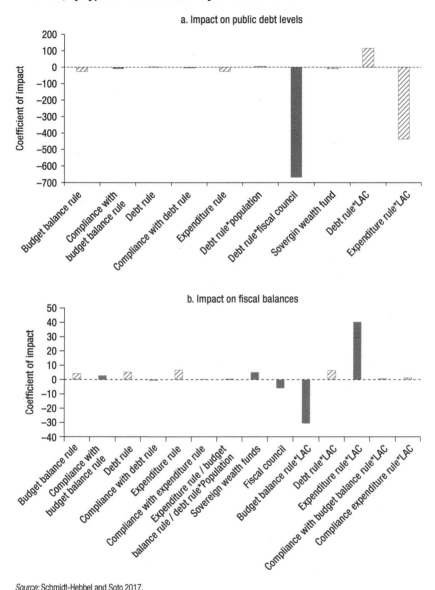

FIGURE O.15: **Impact of Fiscal Rules on Public Debt Levels and Fiscal Balances, by Type of Rule and Country Characteristics**

a. Impact on public debt levels

b. Impact on fiscal balances

Source: Schmidt-Hebbel and Soto 2017.
Note: In panel a, a positive estimated coefficient indicates that rules are effective in improving fiscal discipline (increase budget balance). In panel b, a negative estimated coefficient indicates that rules are effective in reducing the debt level. In both panels, the solid fill indicates statistical significance.

policy makers did not mean for the rules to be truly binding. Unlike in the global sample, in LAC, expenditure rules have a significant, strong effect on improving fiscal balances (figure O.15, panel b). Results suggest that country size does not have a significant impact on the effectiveness of fiscal rules in improving fiscal balances.

Results from this study also indicate that expenditure rules tend to reduce procyclical fiscal policy. Moreover, this effect is stronger when combined with a fiscal council and a sovereign wealth fund. Globally, debt rules, balance rules, and expenditure rules tend to reduce procyclicality, but only expenditure rules have a statistically significant impact on fiscal procyclicality. The presence of a fiscal council or the establishment of a sovereign wealth fund further enhances the smoothing effect of expenditure rules over the cycle. The results show that country size affects the impact of expenditure rules on procyclicality. Among smaller countries, the impact of expenditure rules on expenditure procyclicality is marginally more modest but still significant (table O.4).[15]

Combining fiscal rules intensifies their positive impact on debt sustainability. In particular, the combination of debt rules and expenditure rules favors both the stabilizing role of fiscal policy and its sustainability. Due to the increased prevalence of combined fiscal rules since the global financial crisis of 2008–09, this analysis compares the impact of combinations of rules before and after the crisis. The results

FIGURE O.16: **Impact of Fiscal Rules on 10-Year Expenditure Procyclicality, by Type of Rule and Country Characteristics**

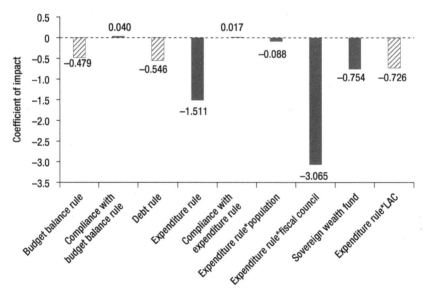

Sources: Schmidt-Hebbel and Soto 2017; Skrok et al. 2017.
Note: A negative estimated coefficient indicates that rules are effective in reducing expenditure procyclicality. The solid fill denotes statistical significance.

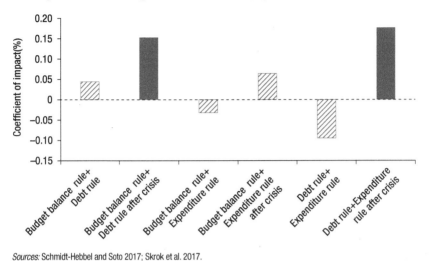

Sources: Schmidt-Hebbel and Soto 2017; Skrok et al. 2017.
Note: A positive coefficient indicates that the fiscal rule strengthens the responsiveness of the primary balance to an increase in the debt stock. The solid fill denotes statistical significance.

TABLE O.4: **Effects of Fiscal Rules: Summary of Findings**

Effect	Balance rules	Debt rules	Expenditure rules
Procyclicality (government expenditures)			
Is procyclicality reduced?	No	No	Yes
Is procyclicality reduced in smaller countries?	No	No	Yes, but less
Is procyclicality reduced in LAC countries?	No	No	Yes, and strongly
Do fiscal councils help to reduce procyclicality?	No	No	Yes
Do sovereign wealth funds help to reduce procyclicality?	No	No	Yes
Procyclicality (fiscal balance)			
Is procyclicality reduced?	Yes, but not significantly	Yes, but not significantly	Yes, but not significantly
Is procyclicality reduced in smaller countries?	No, procyclicality is exacerbated	No	No
Is procyclicality reduced in LAC countries?	Yes, significantly	Yes, significantly	Yes, significantly
Do fiscal councils help to reduce procyclicality?	No	No	No
Do sovereign wealth funds help to reduce procyclicality?	No	No	No

(continued on next page)

TABLE O.4: **Effects of Fiscal Rules: Summary of Findings** *(continued)*

Effect	Budget rules	Debt rules	Expenditure rules
Short-term fiscal sustainability (fiscal balance)			
Do fiscal balances improve?	Yes	Yes	Yes
Do fiscal balances improve in smaller countries?	Yes, but weakly	Yes, but weakly	Yes, but weakly
Do fiscal balances improve in LAC countries?	No, worsen	No	Yes
Do fiscal councils have effect?	Worsens	Worsens	Worsens
Do sovereign wealth funds have effect?	Improves	Improves	Improves
Short-term sustainability (debt)			
Is debt reduced?	No	No	No
Is debt reduced in smaller countries?	Yes	No	No
Is debt reduced in LAC countries?	No, increases debt	No	No
Do fiscal councils help to reduce debt?	No, increases	Yes	Yes
Do sovereign wealth funds have effect?	Reduces	Reduces	Reduces
Long-term sustainability (responsiveness of primary balance)			
Is the primary balance more responsive?	Yes	Yes	No
Is the primary balance more responsive in smaller countries?	No	More responsive	Responsive, but not significantly
Is the primary balance more responsive in LAC countries differently?	No	No	No

Sources: Schmidt-Hebbel and Soto 2017; Skrok et al. 2017.

show that combining debt rules with expenditure rules or debt rules with balance rules enables the primary balance to respond better to changes in indebtedness (figure O.16). Taken together, the results given in figures O.16 and O.17 suggest that combining debt rules and expenditure rules helps to reduce the procyclicality of fiscal policy and to ensure debt sustainability.

Designing Effective Fiscal Rules in Smaller Countries

The design of fiscal rules in smaller countries should take into account their structural features, the patterns of their business cycles, and the types of shocks they frequently face. Identifying which fiscal rule is most appropriate requires a thorough comparison of its effects on fiscal sustainability, output smoothing, and welfare. As these effects are influenced by the characteristics of the business cycle, fiscal rules need to be adapted to the specificities of the business cycle in each country. Indeed, the ability of a fiscal rule to ensure fiscal sustainability and stabilize fluctuations in output will depend on an adequate identification of the sources of volatility, the type of shocks that normally affect the economy, the persistence of shocks, and the amplitude and duration of the business cycle. This study uses analytical models to assess the welfare impact of fiscal rules over time in terms of their ability to promote output stabilization when different types of shocks affect economic activity and government accounts.

As mentioned above, while budget balance rules and debt rules are linked directly to debt sustainability objectives, they tend to amplify the business cycle. By imposing explicit limits on fiscal balances and debt levels, they are expected to exert a direct influence on trends in indebtedness. However, pursuing debt sustainability by imposing only debt or budget balance targets may compromise the ability of fiscal policy to stabilize output over time. Efforts to attenuate the effects of negative shocks can be constrained by fiscal balance targets defined in budget balance rules or by debt rules when actual debt levels are close to the target values.

Structural balance rules are more effective in stabilizing fluctuations in output and smoothing intertemporal consumption in contexts of high volatility. By promoting acyclical fiscal policies, structural balance rules enhance welfare by stabilizing output and consumption. They seem to be an appropriate type of fiscal rule for governments facing substantial volatility in output and highly variable, procyclical public spending because they are particularly effective at isolating spending from fluctuations in revenue and output.

In theory, structural balance rules appear to be the "optimal" fiscal rule for smaller countries facing significant macroeconomic volatility. Given their ability to stabilize the business cycle and smooth household consumption, structural balance rules can strengthen the social insurance effects of fiscal policy. The welfare effects of structural balance rules come from their ability to reduce the procyclicality of public spending; given the pervasive procyclicality observed in smaller countries, fiscal rules that promote acyclicality tend to yield substantial welfare gains. In terms of income distribution effects, structural balance rules are particularly beneficial for low-income households, which are more vulnerable to unemployment, less able to cope with income shocks, and more dependent on government transfers and/or government spending programs. The major advantage of structural balance rules is that by shielding expenditures from temporary fluctuations in revenue, they benefit income groups that are more affected by fluctuations in government spending. By contrast, debt rules and budget balance rules have a much more modest effect on reducing high procyclicality.

However, the benefits of structural balance rules for smaller economies facing highly persistent economic shocks—such as commodity price shocks—are more limited. Using structural balance rules to attenuate persistent shocks may be fiscally unsustainable. If negative commodity price shocks persist (that is, are more "permanent"), the operation of structural balance rules will postpone a necessary fiscal consolidation. In this scenario, if the government accumulates debt to compensate for a more permanent fall in revenue, debt dynamics may become unsustainable. Structural balance rules are even less effective when persistent commodity price shocks have large spillover effects on the nonresource economy, which is the case in smaller countries with limited economic diversification.

In addition, high indebtedness may prevent the adoption of structural balance rules because their functioning in downturns may imply accelerating debt accumulation. Structural balance rules require low levels of indebtedness, which are rare in very small countries. Moreover, adopting structural balance rules may not be feasible for governments with limited access to credit markets. Financial risks increase during economic downturns if the interest rate on debt increases as government debt increases. If interest rate spreads become more sensitive to debt increases, it may not be possible to postpone fiscal consolidation to smooth even a temporary commodity price shock, as accumulating government debt would cause a rapid rise in interest rates, intensifying default risks.

Moreover, structural balance rules have more stringent and complex technical and institutional requirements that may render them less practical for smaller economies in many cases. Implementing, monitoring, and maintaining structural balance rules is technically harder, requiring significant technical capacity. Technical complexities surrounding structural balance rules include difficulties estimating potential output or output gaps, which are sensitive to GDP revisions, revenue elasticities, the size of fiscal multipliers, and the need for real-time macroeconomic monitoring. Further, structural balance rules are difficult to communicate to the public, affecting their transparency from the perspective of citizens, politicians, and other stakeholders. As the targets of structural balance rules are defined on nonobserved (calculated) variables using a large number of assumptions, they are difficult to communicate to general audiences, undermining support for the rule. Due to their nature and complexity, structural balance rules tend to be less transparent than other types of rules. Limited transparency can hamper effective compliance and credibility, as fiscal rules require public scrutiny and a robust political consensus to be supported over time.

An alternative way is to mimic the positive effects generated by a structural balance rule, but with more simplicity and transparency, through the combination of simpler fiscal rules. For example, the adoption of expenditure rules combined with debt rules or expenditure rules combined with budget balance rules can replicate the stabilizing effects of balance budget rules. The welfare gains generated by structural balance rules primarily reflect their ability to reduce expenditure procyclicality. In this sense, expenditure rules can replicate the social insurance effects of structural balance rules. While expenditure rules can make spending acyclical, they are not linked directly to debt sustainability. However, they can trigger the fiscal consolidation necessary to maintain debt sustainability when accompanied by a debt rule or a budget balance rule. The expenditure rule would become the binding constraint during economic upturns, whereas the debt rule (depending on how close the debt-to-GDP ratio is to the ceiling) would become the binding constraint during downturns. Furthermore, a combination of simpler rules may require less administrative capacity and resources to implement.

More flexibility can be obtained by the design and use of escape clauses in the fiscal rule(s) framework. Escape clauses are a critical component of a fiscal rule(s) framework, but they need to be triggered only in the event of truly significant events or shocks. An escape clause could be triggered by a specific idiosyncratic shock—such as a natural disaster, a health pandemic, or a sharp deceleration in GDP growth—or by a commodity shock that substantially affects economic activity and government revenues.[16] Without an escape clause, the expenditure reduction necessary to comply with a budget balance rule or debt rule could potentially exacerbate a shock or deepen an economic downturn. To provide greater flexibility, escape clauses could also allow a temporary deviation from the fiscal rule in the event of the passage of major structural reforms with short-term large, negative fiscal implications. Overall, the lack of an escape clause may force adjustments to the fiscal rules' numerical targets that can undermine the credibility of the fiscal rule framework.

Yet, to preserve credibility, the escape clause should be very well defined, and the transition path toward resumption of the rule should be clearly articulated. This is a critical aspect, as many countries have adopted fiscal rules with ill-defined escape clauses that leave too much scope for government discretion in triggering them or are vague about the resumption path or both. To ensure that the credibility of the rule is not undermined, the escape clause should define (a) the type or types of shocks that can trigger the escape clause, which should be very limited; (b) the exact magnitude of the shock(s), with numerical measures; (c) clear guidelines for the interpretation of events; and (d) a provision that specifies the path back to the fiscal rule, with clearly articulated timing and numerical targets.

Escape clauses are particularly useful in smaller countries more exposed to natural disasters. Regular output or commodity price fluctuations can be better addressed using structural balance rules or a combination of rules. Escape clauses should be triggered only in extraordinary situations that are not recurrent. This is the case for natural disasters or health pandemics with an intense impact. High-impact natural disasters, for example, negatively affect both revenues (through the economic slowdown they trigger) and spending (due to emergency and reconstruction needs). Structural balance rules or a combination of rules also need to have escape clauses if output or price fluctuations are so severe that the stabilization effects of structural balance rules or a combination of debt and expenditure rules are not sufficient. Again, to ensure predictability and credibility, the escape clause should be clearly defined, should be well designed for each specific economy, and should specify a transition path toward resumption of the rule.

The choice of a specific type of rule should respond to analytical and practical principles as well as to initial fiscal conditions. As reflected in table O.5, the choice of a fiscal rule should consider three main criteria: the technical design based on the expected effects of fiscal rules, practical considerations to ensure compliance and effectiveness, and how initial conditions and policy objectives may orient the prioritization of certain objectives over others. From an analytical perspective, ideal rules should ensure fiscal sustainability and provide flexibility to attenuate fluctuations in output and

TABLE O.5: **Criteria for the Selection of Fiscal Rules**

Aspect	Budget balance rules	Structural balance rules	Debt rules	Expenditure rules	Revenue rules
Analytical aspects					
Effect on fiscal sustainability	Strong	Weak	Strong	Medium	Weak
Effect on output stabilization	Negative	Positive	Depending on the actual debt level	Positive, if includes an escape clause	Negative
Welfare and social insurance impacts	Negative	Positive	Negative	Positive	Negative
Type of shocks in which rule is more effective	Highly persistent and asymmetric	Transitory and symmetric	Highly persistent and asymmetric	Transitory and symmetric	Transitory and symmetric
Practical aspects					
Technical and institutional requirements	Low	High	Low	Low	Low
Simplicity and transparency, monitoring and communication	Easy	Difficult	Easy	Easy	Easy
Initial debt conditions					
High debt levels	Suitable	Less suitable	Suitable	Neutral or less suitable (on its own)	Less suitable

Source: World Bank.

consumption. From a practical view, more effective rules are simple to understand, easy to communicate, and easy to implement. The design of fiscal rules should be commensurate with the technical and institutional capacities of the country.

Institutional and technical capacities and the overall fiscal policy framework are key factors affecting compliance with and the effectiveness of fiscal rules. The design and implementation of fiscal rules demand different levels of technical capacity. Appropriate GDP projections, proper identification of business cycles, and sound medium-term fiscal frameworks are critical technical factors underpinning the design of fiscal rules and the definition of target levels. Strong enforcement mechanisms—including the presence of independent fiscal councils that monitor compliance with the rule; sound budgetary and public financial management institutional arrangements, such as the credibility and coverage of the budget; and strong fiscal accounting systems—all favor compliance and effectiveness. Often, the link between the fiscal rules and sovereign wealth funds (stabilization or savings funds) also helps to strengthen the overall framework and the achievement of the fiscal and economic objectives pursued.

In particular, fiscal councils have been shown to be an important institutional tool for improving compliance with and the performance of fiscal rules. Fiscal councils have several functions, from roles related directly to the application of fiscal rules—including oversight of compliance, provision of independent forecasts for applying the rule in annual budget proposals, and assessment of the accuracy of government projections in annual budgets—to broader responsibilities, such as the assessment of fiscal impacts of the policy initiatives, evaluation of medium-term fiscal sustainability, and promotion of public debate on fiscal affairs. While the range of specific functions varies, the main purpose of a fiscal council is to raise the reputational costs of deviating from the rule, manipulating economic projections, and taking unsustainable fiscal stances.

Initial debt levels are also critical in selecting the appropriate fiscal rule. Indeed, initial debt conditions should also guide the selection of rules, since in contexts of high indebtedness, fiscal sustainability and output stabilization are not necessarily compatible and the first objective should be predominant. High debt levels make output smoothing more difficult and costlier. Indeed, the welfare gains from moving to a structural balance rule decrease with debt levels, as higher debt reduces the fiscal space for smoothing shocks and downturns. A negative output shock increases debt-to-GDP ratios, and a small increase or even a decrease in spending may be needed if debt levels and debt service costs are already high. The higher the debt level, the less space there is to apply a structural balance rule because it might be too expensive or there may be no credit to finance the acyclicality of expenditures during downturns.

Well-designed and well-implemented fiscal rules are a good mechanism for all countries, but they are particularly critical for smaller economies. Throughout this study, various findings and lessons from theory and practice are discussed. They clearly show the importance of having well-designed fiscal rules that fit the macroeconomic, external, and other country characteristics. Moreover, with proper establishment, implementation, and compliance, fiscal rules can achieve significantly better fiscal outcomes, less procyclical policies, more output smoothing, and, through these activities, better welfare results for citizens of the country. They also show that design features depend on initial fiscal and debt conditions, country institutional settings, and technical capacities. Obtaining long-term support from key stakeholders and achieving good results also depend on ensuring the simplicity, transparency, and accountability of the fiscal rules framework. This study finds that a large share of the findings and lessons discussed apply roughly similarly to economies of different sizes, although with a few differences in impact and effectiveness between smaller and larger economies. If they are designed and implemented well, fiscal rules are good for all countries, but they are essential for smaller economies, given their special characteristics. Indeed, having a well-designed fiscal rule mechanism as developmental policy is paramount in smaller economies. It seems, however, that policy makers, stakeholders (both local and international), and economic observers have yet to grasp the criticality of the topic for these economies.

Annex 0A. Smaller Countries in the World, by Population Size and Land Area

By Population Size

Region	Below 1.5 million	Below median
East Asia and Pacific	Brunai Darussalam, Fiji, Kiribati, Marshall Islands, Federated States of Micronesia, Palau, Samoa, Solomon Islands, Tonga, Tuvalu	
Europe and Central Asia	Cyprus, Estonia, Greenland, Iceland, Luxembourg, Montenegro	Albania, Armenia, Bosnia and Herzegovina, Croatia, Finland, Georgia, Ireland, Kyrgyz Republic, Latvia, Lithuania, Moldova, North Macedonia, Norway, Slovenia, Turkmenistan
Latin America and the Caribbean	Antigua and Barbuda, The Bahamas, Belize, Barbados, Dominica, Grenada, Guyana, St. Kitts and Nevis, St. Lucia, St. Vincent and the Grenadines, Suriname, Trinidad and Tobago	Costa Rica, Jamaica, Nicaragua, Panama, Paraguay, Uruguay
Middle East and North Africa	Bahrain, Djibouti, Malta, Qatar	Kuwait, Lebanon, Oman, United Arab Emirates
South Asia	Bhutan, Maldives	Afghanistan, Sri Lanka
Sub-Saharan Africa	Cabo Verde, Comoros, Equatorial Guinea, Gabon, The Gambia, Guinea-Bissau, Mauritius, São Tomé and Príncipe, Seychelles, Swaziland	Benin, Botswana, Burundi, Central African Republic, Republic of Congo, Eritrea, Lesotho, Liberia, Mauritania, Namibia, Rwanda, Sierra Leone, Togo

Source: Based on data from World Development Indicators (World Bank).

By Land Area

Region	Below 20,000 square kilometers	Below median
East Asia and Pacific	Brunei Darussalam, China, Fiji, Kiribati, Marshall Islands, Federated States of Micronesia, Palau, Samoa, Singapore, Tonga, Tuvalu, Vanuatu	
Europe and Central Asia	Cyprus, Luxembourg, Montenegro	Albania, Armenia, Belgium, Bosnia and Herzegovina, Croatia, Czech Republic, Denmark, Estonia, Georgia, Ireland, Latvia, Lithuania, Moldova, Netherlands, North Macedonia, Slovak Republic, Slovenia, Switzerland
Latin America and the Caribbean	Antigua and Barbuda, The Bahamas, Barbados, Dominica, Grenada, Jamaica, St. Kitts and Nevis, St. Lucia, St. Vincent and the Grenadines, Trinidad and Tobago	Belize, Costa Rica, Dominican Republic, El Salvador, Haiti, Panama
Middle East and North Africa	Bahrain, Kuwait, Lebanon, Malta, Qatar	Djibouti, Israel, Jordan, United Arab Emirates
South Asia	Maldives	Bangladesh, Bhutan, Sri Lanka
Sub-Saharan Africa	Cabo Verde, Comoros, The Gambia, Mauritius, São Tomé and Príncipe, Seychelles, Swaziland	Benin, Burundi, Equatorial Guinea, Eritrea, Gabon, Ghana , Guinea, Guinea-Bissau, Lesotho, Liberia, Malawi, Rwanda, Senegal, Sierra Leone, Togo, Uganda

Source: Based on data from World Development Indicators (World Bank).

Notes

1. Small countries are defined as having populations below the global median of 4.1 million people; within this group, very small countries have populations below 1.5 million inhabitants. Annex OA contains two tables: one with a list of countries categorized as small and very small by population, and one with a list of economies categorized as such by land area.

2. Regulations to enhance the resilience of physical infrastructure to reduce fatalities and reconstruction costs are also part of precautionary or self-insurance mechanisms.

3. For the interaction of fiscal rules and institutions, see Wyplosz (2005, 2013).

4. These thresholds correspond to the average value over the period 1960–2014. Using average values for population and labor force rather than end-of-period values has the advantage of capturing longer histories of size dynamics. This becomes especially relevant when using thresholds to separate countries into different size groups. For instance, by 2014 several small countries in our data set had transitioned out of the group of small countries after being in it for most of the period. Using average size makes it possible to account for such transitions and to allocate these countries into the small size group. However, not all studies that use population size apply the same threshold values for "small" and "very small" countries. Definitions of "small" range from countries with fewer than 10 million people, of which there were 129 in 2014, to a qualitative definition of modern protected states, which includes just 9 countries.

5. For robustness checks, this study also looks at labor force, land area, and GDP as measures of economic size that are commonly used in the literature.

6. For empirical studies on the characteristics of small economies, see Easterly and Kraay (2000) and Lederman and Lesniak (2017).

7. Control variables include governance; political, economic, and financial risks summarized in the Composite Risk Rating Index from the International Country Risk Guide (ICRG); the presence of fiscal rules; region; commodity exporter status; and exchange rate regimes.

8. Amplitude measures the cumulative growth of GDP during an expansion and contraction. The duration of an expansion is the length (in quarters) between a trough and a peak, while the duration of a contraction is the length between a peak and a trough.

9. Variations of structural balance rules are cyclically adjusted balance rules (CABRs), which correct the effect of the business cycle on the fiscal balance, and over-the-cycle budget balance rules (OCBRs), which require the attainment of a nominal budget balance *on average* over the cycle and are multiyear rather than annual rules.

10. In particular, budget balance rules and structural balance rules.

11. This finding is based on a World Bank data set that includes observed compliance with expenditure rules, balance rules, and debt rules in 63 countries over the 2000–15 period.

12. Budget rigidities are defined as constraints that limit the government's ability to change the level or structure of public spending. These rigidities come in the form of legislative mandates, entitlements, executive provisions, and multiyear commitments, among others. They are often exogenous to government's capacity to mobilize revenue, and they reduce the scope and flexibility to adjust the annual budget.

13. The FRSI was calculated for each fiscal rule based on the methodology proposed by the European Commission using information presented by the IMF (2015).

14. Neither the presence of and nor compliance with expenditure rules has a significant impact on debt sustainability, as this type of rule is expected to have a stronger impact on the procyclicality of government spending.

15. The positive effects of fiscal rules in reducing the procyclicality of fiscal policy and the higher effectiveness of expenditure rules are confirmed when the fiscal balance is used to assess fiscal policy procyclicality.

16. For example, an escape clause could allow a budget balance rule's deficit limit to rise from 1 percent of GDP to 2 percent if the GDP growth rate slows to 1 percent or lower during two consecutive quarters and to 3 percent if the growth rate turns negative for two consecutive quarters. The budget balance rule's deficit limit also could be increased by the size of the cost of addressing the effects of a natural disaster, up to the equivalent of 1 percent of GDP. The escape clause could allow for a deviation of up to three years in the case of a deceleration of GDP, with at least a minimum reduction in the increase of one-third per year or a return to the budget balance rule limit once the rate of growth of GDP has exceeded 1 percent for four consecutive quarters.

References

Debrun, Xavier, Laurent Moulin, Alessandro Turrini, Joaquim Ayuso-i-Casals, and Manmohan S. Kumar. 2008. "Tied to the Mast? National Fiscal Rules in the European Union." *Economic Policy* 23 (54): 299–362.

Debrun, Xavier, Tidiane Kinda, Teresa Curristine, Luc Eyraud, Jason Harris, and Johann Seiwald. 2013. "The Functions and Impact of Fiscal Councils." IMF Policy Paper, International Monetary Fund, Washington, DC.

De la Torre, Augusto, Alain Ize, and Samuel Pienknagura. 2015. *Latin America Treads a Narrow Path to Growth: The Slowdown and Its Macroeconomic Challenges.* LAC Semiannual Report (April). Washington, DC: World Bank.

Easterly, William, and Aart Kraay. 2000. "Small States, Small Problems? Income, Growth, and Volatility in Small States." *World Development* 28 (11): 2013–27.

European Commission. 2009. "Fiscal Rules, Independent Institutions, and Medium-Term Budgetary Frameworks." In *Public Finance in EMU—2009*, part II.2.4, 87–99. Brussels: European Commission.

Fall, Falilou, Debra Bloch, Jean-Marc Fournier, and Peter Hoeller. 2015. "Prudent Debt Targets and Fiscal Frameworks." OECD Economic Policy Paper 15, OECD Publishing, Paris.

Hnatkovska, Viktoria, and Friederike Koehler-Geib. 2017. "Characterizing Business Cycles in Small Economies." Background paper, World Bank, Washington, DC.

Iara, Anna, and Guntram Wolff. 2011. "Rules and Risk in the Euro Area." Bruegel Working Paper 2011/10, Bruegel, Brussels.

IMF (International Monetary Fund). 2015. Fiscal Rules Dataset 1985–2014. IMF, Fiscal Affairs Department, Washington, DC, http://www.imf.org/external/datamapper/fiscalrules/map/map.htm.

IMF (International Monetary Fund). Various years. World Economic Outlook database. Washington, DC: IMF.

Lederman, Daniel, and Justin Lesniak. 2017. "Open and Nimble: Finding Stable Growth in Small Economies." Regional Studies, Office of the Chief Economist for the Latin America and the Caribbean Region, World Bank, Washington, DC.

Marneffe, Wim, Bas Van Aarle, Wouter Van der Wielen, and Lode Vereecl. 2011. "The Impact of Fiscal Rules on Public Finances: Theory and Empirical Evidence for the Euro Area." CESifo DICE Report, vol. 3, CESifo Economic Studies, Oxford University, Oxford.

Schmidt-Hebbel, Klaus, and Raimundo Soto. 2017. "Fiscal Performance, Fiscal Rules, and Country Size." Background paper, World Bank, Washington, DC.

Skrok, Emilia, Jan Gąska, Paulina Hołda, and Friederike N. Koehler-Geib. 2017. "Having or Complying with Fiscal Rules? Insights for Small Countries in LAC." Background paper, World Bank, Washington, DC.

World Bank. Various years. World Development Indicators database. Washington, DC: World Bank.

Wyplosz, Charles. 2005. "Fiscal Policy: Institutions versus Rules." *National Institute Economic Review* 191 (January): 61–78.

Wyplosz, Charles. 2013. "Fiscal Rules: Theoretical Issues and Historical Experiences." In *Fiscal Policy after the Crisis,* edited by Alberto Alesina and Francesco Giavazzi, 496–525. Chicago: University of Chicago Press.

1
Structural Features and Business Cycles in Smaller Countries

Most smaller economies share five key structural features that significantly influence their economic performance and affect the pattern of their business cycles. First, smaller economies tend to be more open to international trade and financial flows. Second, they tend to have relatively undiversified drivers of economic growth and to rely heavily on a single industry or sector. Third, due to diseconomies of scale in the provision of public goods and services, their governments tend to be large relative to their economic size. Fourth, smaller economies are more likely to adopt fixed exchange rate regimes. Fifth and finally, they are likely to suffer especially large losses from natural disasters as a share of gross domestic product (GDP). Due to these characteristics, fiscal policy in smaller countries plays an especially critical role in ensuring resilience to economic shocks and reducing volatility while preserving fiscal sustainability.

Due to these structural characteristics, smaller economies exhibit greater average fluctuations in GDP growth, with deeper economic contractions and shorter expansions than larger countries. They tend to have more volatile, less procyclical private consumption and investment but also more volatile, more procyclical external and fiscal balances. Smaller economies are more vulnerable to terms-of-trade and output shocks and have higher, more volatile unemployment rates than large economies. Smaller economies have experienced lower and more volatile growth during the last 15 years. This trend has been particularly marked in the very small countries in Latin America and the Caribbean (LAC), which are highly exposed to greater exogenous volatility involving frequent and more intense natural disasters that have affected economic activity and pressured government spending and undermined their revenue bases. Understanding the interaction between sources of volatility and structural characteristics is key for the design of fiscal rules, particularly those aimed at attenuating economic fluctuations.

Introduction

This chapter examines the structural features of many smaller countries that are relevant for the design of fiscal rules. The chapter highlights similarities among smaller countries, in terms of both their structural characteristics and their recent economic performance, as well as significant differences between smaller and larger countries. While smaller countries are heterogeneous, they share common structural characteristics and business cycle features. These structural and business cycle features are linked not only to economic size but also to other factors, including their level of economic development, commodity exporter status, location, and other economic characteristics. After controlling for some of these factors, this chapter shows that economic size has a significant role in shaping the key structural characteristics and economic performance of smaller economies.

Recognizing their heterogeneity, this analysis distinguishes "small" and "very small" economies, which are defined as having populations below 4.1 million and 1.5 million, respectively. Threshold values for smaller countries are somewhat arbitrary in the literature. Definitions of "small countries" range between countries with below 10 million inhabitants (129 countries, as of 2014) and a qualitative definition of modern protected states (just 9 countries) (see Dumienski 2014). In this chapter and throughout this study, "smaller countries" are defined as the 86 countries with average populations below 4.1 million during 1960–2014, which is the median of the global sample for this period (table 1.1).[1] Of these countries, 51 are considered "very small," as they have populations of fewer than 1.5 million.[2] The LAC region is home to 18 small countries, or 21 percent of the world's small countries, and to 12 "very small" countries, or 24 percent of all "very small" countries worldwide.

This chapter has three sections. The first outlines the main structural characteristics of smaller economies and provides evidence that these characteristics are related to economic size by comparing them to the characteristics observed in larger countries. The second section compares the patterns of the business cycle in small economies

---

TABLE 1.1: **Small and Very Small Countries in LAC and Non-LAC Regions, by Population Size and Land Area**

Region	Population		Land area	
	Small: Below median	Very small: 1.5 million	Small: Below median	Very small: Below 20,000 square kilometers
LAC	18	12	16	10
Non-LAC	68	39	70	32
Total	**86**	**51**	**86**	**42**

Source: Calculations based on data from World Development Indicators (World Bank).
Note: The sample median for population is 4.1 million. The sample median for land area is 10,000 square kilometers.

with those in larger economies and assesses the effects of economic size. The third section summarizes the main findings, highlighting possible implications for the design of fiscal rules.

Structural Characteristics of Small Economies

Small economies share several structural features (figure 1.1):

- *Greater trade openness.* With small domestic markets preventing the formation of economies of scale, small economies need to expose themselves to international markets, which explains their greater openness to trade.
- *Low economic diversification.* Smallness and diseconomies of scale result in high economic concentration and reliance on the exports of a few goods or services, which lead to an undiversified set of drivers of economic growth.

FIGURE 1.1: **Characteristics of Small Countries**

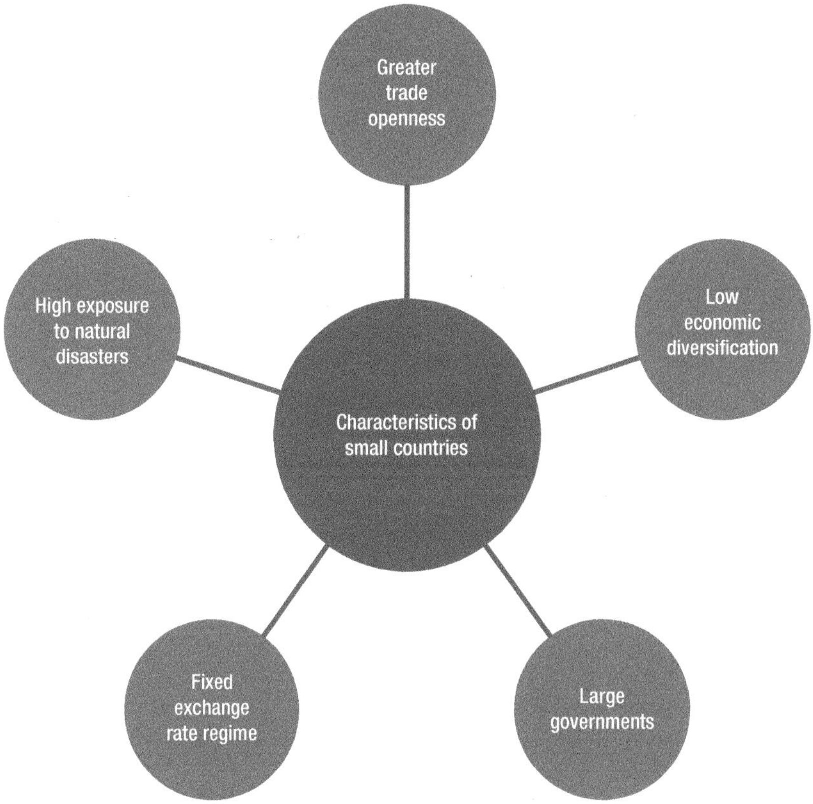

Source: World Bank.

CHAPTER 1: STRUCTURAL FEATURES AND BUSINESS CYCLES IN SMALLER COUNTRIES   45

- *Large governments in relative terms.* Small countries have higher unit costs for the provision of public goods and services, which tend to result in higher ratios of expenditures to GDP and larger public sector wage bills.

- *Fixed exchange rate regimes.* Small economies are more inclined to adopt fixed exchange rate regimes because of the high fixed costs of operating a domestic monetary policy and their vulnerability to changes in terms of trade.

- *High exposure to natural disasters.* The economies of small countries are generally more susceptible to the impact of natural disasters and climate change and have higher economic costs relative to GDP.

Greater Openness to Trade and International Financing

Small countries are more reliant on foreign trade because of their small markets for domestic goods and factors of production. International markets absorb their domestic production, provide imports to satisfy domestic demand, finance their investment needs, and employ a large part of their citizens. Many small states have little agricultural land and few energy resources, making them especially reliant on imported food and fuel. They also tend to be more dependent on external flows, such as foreign direct investment (FDI), remittances, and official financing. Moreover, many small countries have shallow financial sectors, and their export sectors are often financed by foreign capital. Finally, their small domestic consumer markets tend to encourage dependence on imports rather than investment in local production. The small labor markets of smaller states also help to explain their higher rates of labor force migration and larger share of remittances to gross national income (GNI).

As a result, global economic conditions greatly influence the growth and development of small economies. Between 2000 and 2015, the sum of exports and imports represented an average of 111.8 percent of aggregate GDP for small economies, compared with an average of just 73 percent for large economies (figure 1.2, panel a). FDI and remittances as a share of GDP were almost twice as high in small as in large states, and very small economies were especially reliant on FDI. Except for remittances, there were few differences in openness between LAC countries, both large and small, and countries in the rest of the world (figure 1.2, panel b).

Low Economic Diversification and High Concentration of Exports

Many small economies have limited potential for economic diversification. On the one hand, large economies are likely to possess a wide range of resources, abundant productive factors, and large consumer markets, enabling them to leverage economies of scale and agglomeration and to develop complex value chains. On the other hand, small countries often lack the resources to diversify their economies and instead focus on a narrow set of activities in which they enjoy a comparative advantage.[3]

Structural Features of Countries in LAC and the World, by Country Size, 2000–15

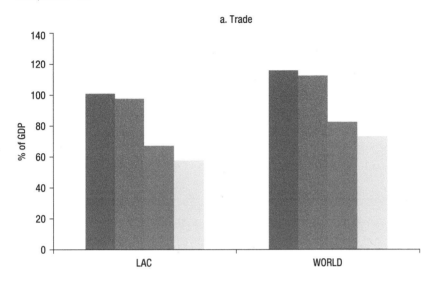

a. Trade

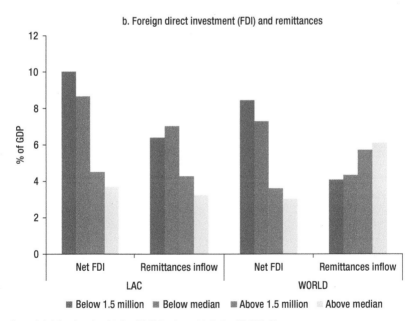

b. Foreign direct investment (FDI) and remittances

■ Below 1.5 million ■ Below median ■ Above 1.5 million ░ Above median

Source: Calculations based on data from World Development Indicators (World Bank).

Smaller economies have less diversified export baskets, exports destination markets, and lower rates of export growth than large economies. The Herfindahl-Hirschman Index (HHI), which measures the composition of exports per destination markets and products, shows that smaller economies tend to rely more heavily on a narrower range of export products.[4] For the period 1995–2013, smaller and very small economies had average HHI scores for concentration of export markets and products and lower rates of export growth—0.29 and 0.32, respectively—compared with an average of 0.23 for larger countries (figure 1.3). Even though this pattern is also observed in LAC, small LAC countries have more diversified exports than larger LAC economies in terms of destination markets.[5] Due in part to their high levels of export concentration, small states tend to have lower average rates of export growth, as their undiversified economies and limited resources inhibit them from developing new export sectors (Favaro 2017).

Large Governments in Relative Terms

The size of government in small countries, particularly in very small economies, tends to be large due to indivisibility and diseconomies of scale in the provision of public goods and services.[6] Traditional public goods—such as foreign affairs,

FIGURE 1.3: **Concentration of Exports in LAC and the World, by Country Size, 1995–2013**

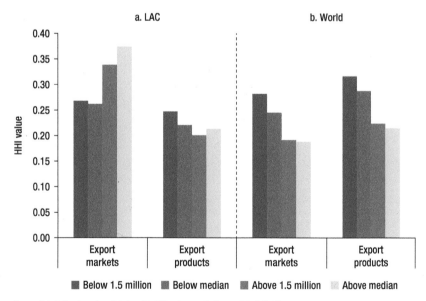

Source: Calculations based on data from World Development Indicators (World Bank).
Note: HHI = Herfindahl-Hirschman Index.

national defense, law enforcement, legislatures, justice administration, and economic management—need to be provided independently of the size of a country's population. Owing to indivisibility and high fixed costs, the unit cost of providing public services—such as infrastructure, energy, education, health, and public security—is generally higher in small economies.

Indeed, government spending relative to GDP is substantially higher in smaller economies. Between 2000 and 2015, public sector spending represented an average of 34.7 percent of GDP in smaller countries and 37.5 percent in very small ones, well above the average of 30.7 percent observed in larger countries. Government consumption also tends to be higher in smaller countries, while investment does not have significant differences between smaller and larger countries. In the LAC region, government spending levels are generally lower than in the rest of the world and differences between smaller and larger countries in the size of government are less acute (figure 1.4).

Fixed Exchange Rate Regimes

Smaller countries are more likely to adopt less flexible exchange rate regimes, and this likelihood is more pronounced in small LAC countries. The use of fixed or pegged exchange rate regimes may be related to the high unitary costs of providing public goods, suggesting that autonomous monetary management institutions may be costly. Moreover, given the high openness and shallowness of domestic financial markets, the stabilizing role of monetary policy may be limited. Many small

FIGURE 1.4: **Government Spending as Percentage of GDP in LAC and the World, by Country Size, 2000–15**

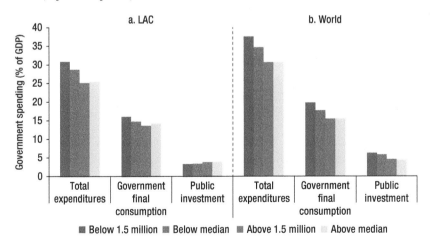

Sources: Calculations based on data from World Development Indicators (World Bank) and World Economic Outlook (IMF).

countries have adopted less flexible exchange rate regimes with the aim of bolstering their integration with global financial markets by stabilizing currency fluctuations and increasing investor confidence. In smaller countries, fixed exchange regimes seem to be more effective for financial and monetary stability, which are hard for autonomous monetary policy institutions to ensure. However, more fixed exchange rates prevent governments from using monetary policy to support output stabilization and may heighten cyclical volatility, making fiscal policy even more important. Between 2000 and 2015, only 16.8 percent of large countries used fixed exchange rates compared with more than 40 percent of small states and almost 60 percent of very small states. Small economies in LAC were especially likely to peg their currencies: almost 45 percent of small economies and a full 70 percent of very small states used fixed exchange rates (figure 1.5).

Exposure to Natural Disasters

Small countries in general are especially vulnerable to natural disasters, and costs for these events are relatively higher in smaller LAC countries. Although large countries experience similar exposure to environmental hazards—such as hurricanes, tsunamis, and the effects of climate change—these hazards have a great impact on small countries relative to their economic size. This situation is particularly problematic for small islands that rely on their natural resources

FIGURE 1.5: Percentage of Countries with Fixed Exchange Rate Regimes in LAC and the World, by Country Size, 2000–15

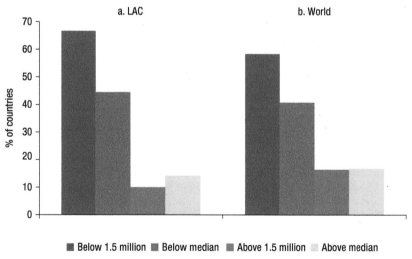

Sources: Calculations based on data from World Development Indicators (World Bank) and World Economic Outlook (International Monetary Fund).

for tourism. Between 2000 and 2015, the economic losses caused by natural disasters were 130 percent greater in small than in large countries. Many of LAC's very small countries are located in the Caribbean basin, which is prone to devastating hurricanes and protracted droughts, and in Central America, which is vulnerable to seismic events and extreme weather conditions. The relative economic losses that natural disasters have inflicted on small countries in LAC are 400 percent higher than those inflicted on large countries and losses for very small countries are a staggering 620 percent higher (figure 1.6).

The structural characteristics outlined in this section are robustly associated with economic size. After controlling for economic development, geographic region, and other socioeconomic variables, the relationships between economic size, and export diversification, size of governments, exchange rate regimes, and vulnerability to natural disasters, remain strong and significant (table 1.2). The linear relationship between economic size and openness, diversification, size of government, exchange rate regime, and exposure to natural hazards suggests that these structural features are also present in larger countries, though to a lesser degree than in smaller countries. This implies that the findings of this study can also be relevant to larger countries and that policy recommendations may also be applied in them.

FIGURE 1.6: **Value of Losses Due to Natural Disasters in LAC and the World, by Country Size, 2000–15**

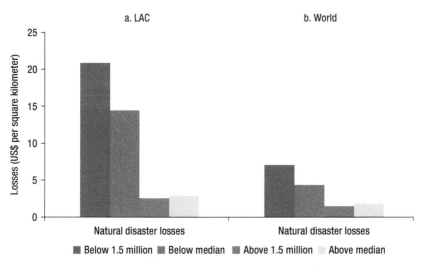

Sources: Calculations based on data from World Development Indicators (World Bank) and EM-DAT (CRED).

Economic Size and Structural Features of Smaller Economies

Dependent variable	Measured by population			Measured by land area		
	Continuous Log (pop)	Dummy < median	Dummy < 1.5 million	Continuous Ln (area)	Dummy < median	Dummy < 20,000 square kilometers
Openness						
Trade openness as measured by (X+M)/GDP	−9.77*** (1.56)	38.69*** (6.40)	35.09*** (9.83)	−8.37*** (1.57)	32.00*** (6.41)	35.87*** (10.62)
Remittances as % of GDP	−0.931*** (0.233)	3.794*** (1.117)	2.707* (1.394)	−1.004*** (0.197)	4.060*** (1.097)	4.141*** (1.308)
Foreign direct investment (net) as % of GDP	−1.379*** (0.487)	4.926*** (1.504)	6.119** (2.900)	−1.388** (0.598)	4.471*** (1.445)	7.476** (3.161)
Export concentration						
HHI for market destination	−0.0213*** (0.00495)	0.0541** (0.0214)	0.0775*** (0.0281)	−0.0124*** (0.00410)	0.0689*** (0.0205)	0.0343 (0.0262)
HHI for products	−0.0197** (0.00804)	0.0622* (0.0364)	0.0984** (0.0457)	0.00270 (0.00746)	0.00115 (0.0371)	0.0484 (0.0491)
Number of trade partners	13.32*** (0.678)	−40.53*** (4.164)	−52.38*** (5.088)	8.725*** (0.813)	−34.75*** (4.484)	−46.55*** (6.570)
Number of export products	77.55*** (4.125)	−240.8*** (25.20)	−301.8*** (28.60)	48.27*** (4.791)	−171.0*** (27.69)	−269.6*** (36.92)
Government size						
Government consumption as % of GDP	−0.992** (0.467)	2.248 (1.508)	4.988* (2.713)	−0.494 (0.337)	2.145 (1.891)	3.636 (3.018)
Total government expenditures as % of GDP	−1.876*** (0.595)	3.796** (1.644)	7.493*** (2.212)	−1.243** (0.519)	4.088** (1.769)	5.819** (2.598)
Exposure to natural disasters						
Cost of natural disaster damage per capita conditional on having experienced a natural disaster	−3.205* (1.814)	6.279 (4.367)	14.70* (8.545)	−3.293** (1.614)	8.251* (4.306)	19.95* (10.61)
Cost of natural disaster damage per 1,000 square kilometers of land area	−1.050 (0.897)	2.361 (2.447)	5.034 (3.865)	−1.243 (0.800)	3.901 (2.617)	7.350 (4.952)

Source: World Bank.

Note: HHI = Herfindahl-Hirschman Index, ln = land, Log = logarithm, M = imports, X = exports.

*** $p < .01$ ** $p < .05$ * $p < .10$.

Business Cycles in Smaller Economies

Due to their distinctive structural features, smaller economies experience greater volatility and have more pronounced business cycles. First, smaller countries are more open to international trade, which makes them more susceptible to external shocks. Exogenous sources of volatility, such as terms-of-trade fluctuations, tend to be exacerbated in smaller countries given their higher trade openness. Second, factors of production cannot be relocated easily across economic sectors or regions when production and exports are concentrated in a few sectors, which makes smaller economies less able to accommodate shocks.[7] Third, smaller countries tend to have relatively larger governments, which means that the impact of volatility and procyclicality in government expenditures and revenues on economic activity is expected to be stronger. Moreover, smaller countries tend to use fixed exchange rate regimes, leaving the full duty of output stabilization to fiscal policy. Fourth, weather-related shocks and natural disasters not only are more frequent but also have a greater economic impact on smaller countries. All of these structural characteristics indicate that business cycles are likely to be more pronounced in smaller economies.

Indeed, differences between the business cycles in small and large economies are significant, and they remain significant even when other structural and policy variables are considered.[8] This section demonstrates that business cycles are more volatile in small economies than in larger ones. Moreover, the length and amplitude of GDP cycles are significantly different between the two groups of countries. This section identifies the sources of volatility and shows that small countries are more susceptible to terms-of-trade shocks than larger countries. The analysis shows that differences in the business cycles of smaller and larger economies persist when controlling for level of development, commodity exporter status, exchange rate regime, presence of fiscal rules, and geographic location.

Based on a data set for 138 countries spanning the period from 1960 to 2014, the analysis of the differences between smaller and larger economies uses two complementary approaches to evaluate the effects of economic size on characteristics of the business cycle.[9] The first contrasts the variable of interest in "smaller" versus "larger" countries by testing the significance of differences between the two discrete groups. This approach uses two population thresholds: 1.5 million, and the sample median of 4.1 million. The second approach uses a continuous population variable in regression analyses to estimate the effect of economic size on business cycle characteristics. The analyses rely on simple ordinary least squares regressions of the characteristics of the business cycle on economic size using the control variables mentioned above, the level of development proxied by the International Country Risk Guide (ICRG) Index, and other structural and policy variables such as commodity-exporting status, exchange rate regimes, presence of fiscal rules, and regional dummies.[10]

Volatility of GDP, GNI, Consumption, Investment, External Balances, and Unemployment

GDP and GNI are more volatile in smaller economies.[11] The average values of the standard deviation of GDP and GNI are significantly higher for smaller than for larger countries. This is the case when comparing small versus large countries using the two thresholds (table 1.3, panel a), but also when using a continuous population variable reflecting economic size (table 1.3, panel b). Higher volatility in smaller countries persists when introducing various control variables (second and third columns of table 1.3, panel b).

Smaller countries also experience heightened volatility in other macroeconomic variables, including private and government consumption and total investment and external sector balance. Higher volatility likely reflects their limited ability to absorb shocks and provide insurance across sectors as well as their less developed automatic fiscal stabilizers. This finding is robust when exogenous volatility measured by average standard deviations between small and large countries is compared and also when the exogenous volatility measure is regressed on economic size. Furthermore, the results remain robust when controlling for level of development. The effect of economic size on volatility remains consistent when all control variables are included. Similarly, total investment is more volatile in small economies. Government investment is also more volatile in smaller states, but the difference between smaller and large countries is not significant. Smaller countries have more volatile external balances due to their less diversified structures of production and exports. Even though there are no significant differences between larger and smaller countries in terms-of-trade volatility, smaller economies have more volatile trade and current account balances. This volatility could be linked to their greater trade and financial openness, but also to their higher export concentration. Smaller countries also have higher levels and volatility of unemployment, as shown in figure 1.7.[12] This finding is in line with the higher volatility of GDP and stronger concentration of production and exports in smaller economies. These insights are highly relevant for the formulation of fiscal policy because smaller economies have a greater need than larger economies to create fiscal buffers against economic shocks to protect their populations.

Business Cycles: Duration and Amplitude

Business cycles are more asymmetric in smaller countries: cyclical contractions are deeper in smaller than in larger countries, while expansions are of similar amplitude but shorter duration (table 1.4). The average depth of economic contractions is deeper in smaller countries, with an average cumulative drop in GDP equal to 7 percent in small countries versus 5 percent in large countries.[13] Moreover, the amplitude of expansions is the same in the two groups of countries, equal to 29 percent, while the average duration of economic expansions is shorter in small countries (17.6 quarters) relative to large countries (23.9 quarters), and the difference is statistically significant at 5 percent.[14]

TABLE 1.3: **Volatility and Economic Size, by Country Size, 1960–2014**

a. Difference by population threshold

Indicator	Below 1.5 million	Above 1.5 million	Difference	Below median	Above median	Difference
GDP	4.94	4.67	−0.27	5.51	4.16	−1.35***
GNI	7.96	4.01	−3.95***	6.97	3.72	−3.25***
Private consumption	1.78	1.25	0.53***	1.70	1.19	0.51***
Government consumption	2.00	1.78	0.22	2.09	1.70	0.39
Total investment	3.28	3.34	−0.06	3.74	3.17	0.58**
Private investment	6.08	5.23	0.85	5.93	5.13	0.80
Government investment	7.29	6.58	0.71	6.72	6.68	0.04
Current account / GDP	5.29	3.63	1.66	6.16	2.70	3.46***
Trade balance / GDP	7.62	3.49	4.13***	6.56	3.17	3.39***

b. Regression of volatilities on continuous population size (ln pop)

Indicator	Baseline (1)	Controlling by economic development (2)	With all controls (3)
GDP	−0.06***	−0.06***	−0.10***
GNI	−0.17***	−0.17***	−0.16***
Private consumption	−0.08***	−0.09***	−0.06
Government consumption	−0.01	−0.03	−0.07*
Total investment	−0.06**	−0.06**	−0.08***
Private investment	−0.06	−0.05	−0.09
Government investment	−0.04	−0.04	0.11
Current account / GDP	−0.18***	−0.18***	−0.20***
Trade balance / GDP	−0.21***	−0.24***	−0.22***

Source: Hnatkovska and Koehler-Geib 2018a.
Note: Volatility is measured as standard deviation, by population size. Economic size is measured using both a continuous variable and two groups of "small" countries: those with populations below 1.5 million and those with populations below the sample median. Hnatkovska and Koehler-Geib (2018a) also present results for land area and labor force measures. These results are robust. The analysis is based on yearly data for 138 countries with data from 1960 to 2014.
*** $p < .01$ ** $p < .05$ * $< .10$.

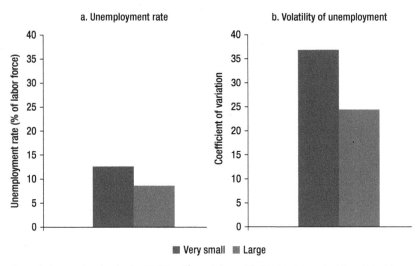

FIGURE 1.7: **Unemployment Levels and Volatility, by Country Size**

a. Unemployment rate

b. Volatility of unemployment

■ Very small ■ Large

Sources: Aguirre 2017, based on data from World Development Indicators (World Bank) and International Financial Statistics (International Monetary Fund).

Note: Very small countries are defined as countries with populations less than 1.5 million. The figure shows group averages using annual World Development Indicator data. Data from 49 small countries and 167 large countries. Standard deviation using quarterly data, International Finance Statistics. Data from 7 very small countries and 65 large countries.

TABLE 1.4: **Duration and Amplitude of Expansions and Contractions of GDP, by Country Size**

Indicator	Number of observations	Duration (in quarters)		Amplitude	
		Mean	Standard deviation	Mean	Standard deviation
Small					
Expansions	22	17.62	10.0	0.29	0.21
Contractions	22	4.3	2.26	−0.07	0.06
Large					
Expansions	47	23.87	11.63	0.29	0.16
Contractions	46	4.38	2.71	−0.05	0.05

Source: Hnatkovska and Koehler-Geib 2018a.

Note: Small countries are defined as having populations below 4.151 million. Large countries are defined as having populations equal to or above 4.151 million. Based on quarterly data for 69 countries (39 high-income and 30 low- and middle-income) from 1960 to 2015.

TABLE 1.5: **Variance Decomposition of GDP Volatility, by Population Size**

Variable	Small countries Number of countries	Mean	Large countries Number of countries	Mean	Mean difference
(log) Terms of Trade	5	0.15	16	0.077	−0.074
US Treasury bill rate	5	0.044	16	0.135	0.091**
(log) US GDP	5	0.055	16	0.156	0.101
(log) Government expenditures	5	0.108	16	0.086	−0.022
Trade balance to GDP	5	0.023	16	0.056	0.033*
Real interest rate	5	0.051	16	0.035	−0.017
(log) GDP	5	0.54	16	0.397	−0.143
(log) Effective real exchange rate	5	0.028	16	0.058	0.03

Source: Hnatkovska and Koehler-Geib 2018a.
Note: Based on quarterly data for 69 countries (39 high-income and 30 low- and middle-income) from 1960 to 2015. Due to limitations of the sample size, very small countries are included in the group of small countries. log = logarithm.
** $p < .05$ * $< .10$.

The duration and amplitude of economic upturns and downturns are important when designing fiscal rules aimed at attenuating economic fluctuations. More volatile GDP and GNI with deeper contractions and shorter expansions have important implications for the definition of numerical targets for structural or cyclically adjusted balances. In particular, to compensate for deficits during deeper downturns, positive balances during shorter upturns should be sufficiently high to support the build-up of considerable buffers to counteract prolonged economic downturns.

Identifying the Sources of Volatility

Terms-of-trade shocks have stronger effects in smaller countries than in larger ones.[15] Across all countries, on average, about 22 percent of the overall GDP volatility is driven by external shocks, including shocks to the world real interest rate (proxied by the US Treasury bill rate) and shocks to foreign demand conditions (proxied by US GDP). Domestic shocks account for the remaining 78 percent and include shocks to own GDP, government expenditures, domestic real interest rates, and exchange rates. The effects of country size on variance decompositions are particularly pronounced in low- and middle-income countries. While small low- and middle-income countries are more prone to domestic output shocks, large low- and middle-income countries are more prone to shocks to the world's interest rate and real exchange rate. Adding terms-of-trade shocks to the set of external factors in the estimation reduces the sample size due to limitations in the availability of data. When including terms-of-trade shocks, the contribution of external shocks in overall GDP volatility increases, especially in small economies (table 1.5). In smaller countries, the contribution of terms-of-trade shocks to overall GDP volatility reaches 15 percent versus just 7.7 percent in large economies. These findings are consistent with the greater degree of export concentration and greater openness to trade in smaller countries.[16]

Summary of Findings

The distinctive structural features of smaller countries create fiscal and macroeconomic patterns that are distinct from those of their larger counterparts. Smaller economies tend to be more open to international trade and more reliant on a limited range of productive activities and export sectors. Their governments are often large relative to the size of their economies, and they are more likely to use fixed exchange rates. Small countries also tend to be more vulnerable to the impact of natural disasters. These structural characteristics result in more intense macroeconomic volatility, more pronounced business cycles, and greater fiscal procyclicality. Smaller countries tend to experience shorter expansions and deeper recessions, are especially prone to terms-of-trade shocks, and are more likely to suffer from fiscal instability and unsustainable debt dynamics.

Moreover, the recent economic performance of smaller countries underscores the impact of their structural characteristics. Throughout the 2000s, small countries exhibited lower and more volatile GDP growth than their larger peers. The unstable fiscal balances of many smaller countries reflected their especially heavy reliance on trade taxes, which left their budgets highly sensitive to external shocks. Smaller countries also experienced larger average debt-to-GDP ratios, as more procyclical patterns of expenditures exacerbated wider fiscal deficits.

In this context, fiscal policy plays a larger role in dealing with volatility, resilience, and sustainability in smaller countries. Due to the particular characteristics and outcomes of smaller economies and the more extensive use of less flexible exchange rate regimes, fiscal policy becomes even more critical. Fiscal policy can exert a central role in saving resources in good times that can then be used in downturns to stabilize more frequent and deeper fluctuations in output. This implies the need for well-crafted fiscal mechanisms.

Well-designed fiscal rules can thus be critical to smoothing macroeconomic fluctuations and stabilizing consumption over time, while maintaining fiscal sustainability in smaller countries. However, they need to be informed by the features of their business cycle. The strong fluctuations in GDP experienced by smaller countries call for giving fiscal policy an enhanced role in stabilization and for pursuing acyclical fiscal rules to smooth fluctuations and prevent the exacerbation of GDP cycles. At the same time, the asymmetric nature of economic cycles in smaller countries, with deeper and longer recessions, also suggests that output-stabilizing fiscal rules need to be designed carefully to prevent unsustainable debt dynamics. In particular, building sufficient buffers in shorter expansions to be used in longer and deeper recessions may require additional fiscal efforts reflected in higher fiscal balances in upturns than the ones required in contexts where business cycles are symmetric.

Notes

This chapter is based on three background papers prepared for this study: Favaro (2017) and Hnatkovska and Koehler-Geib (2018a, 2018b).

1. Most of the assessments presented in this chapter refer to population, but labor force and land area are also used. Results shown in this report are robust to these alternative criteria for smallness.

2. The 1.5 million threshold is the most common in the literature and is used by the World Bank, the International Monetary Fund, and others to define small states. However, there is no agreed-on definition of a "small state." For instance, work by the Commonwealth Secretariat and the World Bank on small states includes larger economies, such as Botswana, Jamaica, Lesotho, and Namibia; they argue that these countries have characteristics similar to those of small states. The United Nations includes high-income countries, such as Malta and Singapore, in its categorization of small island states as well as countries such as Guinea-Bissau and Guyana that, while not islands, have characteristics similar to those observed in countries with populations below the 1.5 million threshold.

3. See World Bank, http://www.worldbank.org/en/country/smallstates/overview.

4. The HHI is calculated as the sum of the squares of the share of each export market or export products in total exports. Higher values indicate higher export concentration or less economic diversification.

5. This pattern is due to their highly diversified destination markets (demand) for tourism services, the most important export of small Caribbean countries.

6. For a discussion of the challenges posed by the lack of economies of scale in providing public services and possible solutions, see Favaro (2008).

7. For empirical studies on the characteristics of small economies, see Easterly and Kraay (2000) and Lederman and Lesniak (2017).

8. This analysis draws primarily on Hnatkovska and Koehler-Geib (2018a, 2018b), who analyze the characteristics of business cycles and sources of volatility in small economies. Hnatkovska and Koehler-Geib (2018a) also analyze the persistence of fluctuations, but this chapter does not present their findings because the persistence of variables of interest does not vary significantly by country size.

9. To check the robustness of the results, three measures of size are used: population, land area, and labor force. The results reported here refer to economic size measured by population. Results using land area and labor force as measures of economic size are consistent with findings using population and can be found in Hnatkovska and Koehler-Geib (2018a).

10. Previous literature has identified the level of development as an important determinant of business cycle characteristics. Examples include Aguiar and Gopinath (2007), Calderón and Fuentes (2010), and Neumeyer and Perri (2005).

11. GNI is more volatile than GDP, which is in line with the understanding that net flows of foreign income are more variable in small than in large countries.

12. The small number of observations on unemployment rates precluded undertaking regression analysis to demonstrate this pattern.

13. To compare the duration and amplitude of business cycles experienced by small and large economies, a nonparametric approach was used to date business cycles. Based on a quarterly data set of 39 high-income and 30 low- and middle-income countries for which quarterly GDP data are available from 1960 to 2015, the analysis relies on a nonparametric approach to decompose trend and cyclical components of macro variables developed by Bry and Boschan (1971) for monthly data and adapted to quarterly data by Harding and Pagan (2002). This methodology dates business cycles by determining the turning points of the series, thus partitioning them into expansion and contraction phases. The resulting business cycles are characterized by the duration and amplitude of expansions and contractions. The analysis then compares those characteristics between small and large economies.

14. These results for small versus large countries echo the findings in the literature that compare business cycles in developing and developed countries. For instance, using Bry and Boschan's (1971) procedure to determine the turning points in a GDP series for 15 developing countries, Rand and Tarp (2002) show that the average length of the business cycle for developing countries is smaller (between 7 and 18 quarters, or 4.5 years). Other studies that use different dating procedures show no significant difference in the duration of business cycles between developing countries and developed countries (see Male 2010, among others). Yet others show more mixed evidence. For instance, Calderón and Fuentes (2010) find that on some dimensions, such as the duration of contractions, developing countries and developed countries are similar, while on other dimensions, such as the duration of expansions, they differ, with developing countries experiencing shorter expansions, on average.

15. The data set for sources of volatility is also quarterly and covers the period from 1960 to 2015. The analysis relies on individual country and panel structural vector auto regressions. These models are used to assess the role played by various internal and external shocks in each country or group of countries. The analyzed shocks contain domestic shocks such as shocks to government expenditures, trade balance, real interest rate, real exchange rate, and GDP. The analysis of the sources of volatility uses structural vector autoregression for each country in the sample and variance decompositions, conditional on various country characteristics, such as size, development level, institutional quality, and presence of fiscal rules.

16. Several studies have estimated the economic impact of natural disasters. Auffret (2003) assessed the impact of catastrophic events on macroeconomic variables for a sample of 16 countries (6 from the Caribbean region and 10 from Latin America) and found that these events do not have a negative impact on output, consumption, and investment growth. Raddatz (2007) measured the contribution of natural disasters in fluctuations of output and found that natural disasters have a negative short-run impact on output. Cavallo and Noy (2009) reviewed available data sources and summarized the economic literature on the impact of natural disasters. However, assessments of the impact of natural disasters on macroeconomic volatility are scarce.

References

Aguiar, Mark, and Gita Gopinath. 2007. "Emerging Market Business Cycles: The Cycle Is the Trend." *Journal of Political Economy* 115 (11): 69–102.

Aguirre, Alvaro. 2017. "Welfare Effects of Fiscal Rules with Heterogeneous Agents in Small Open Economies." Background paper, World Bank, Washington, DC. http://documents.worldbank .org/curated/en/299961597691885453/Welfare-Effects-of-Fiscal-Rules-with-Heterogeneous -Agents-in-Small-Open-Economies.

Auffret, Philippe. 2003. "High Consumption Volatility: The Impact of Natural Disasters?" Policy Research Working Paper 2962, World Bank, Washington, DC.

Bry, Gerhard, and Charlotte Boschan. 1971. "Cyclical Analysis of Time Series: Selected Procedures and Computer Programs." NBER Technical Paper 20, National Bureau of Economic Research, Cambridge, MA.

Calderón, César, and Rodrigo Fuentes. 2010. "Characterizing the Business Cycles of Emerging Economies." Policy Research Working Paper 5343, World Bank, Washington, DC.

Cavallo, Eduardo, and Ilan Noy. 2009. "The Economics of Natural Disasters: A Survey." IDB Working Paper 124, Inter-American Development Bank, Washington, DC.

CRED (Centre for Research on the Epidemiology of Disasters). Various years. EM-DAT: The OFDA/CRED International Disaster database. Brussels: Catholic University of Leuven, Leuven.

Dumienski, Zbigniew. 2014. "Microstates as Modern Protected States: Towards a New Definition of Micro-Statehood." Occasional Paper, Institute of International Affairs, Centre for Small States Studies, University of Auckland, Auckland.

Easterly, William, and Aart Kraay. 2000. "Small States, Small Problems? Income, Growth, and Volatility in Small States." *World Development* 28 (11): 2013–27.

Favaro, Edgardo. 2008. *Small States, Smart Solutions: Improving Connectivity and Increasing the Effectiveness of Public Services.* Direction in Development: Public Sector Governance. Washington, DC: World Bank.

Favaro, Edgardo. 2017. "Benefits and Costs of Implementing Fiscal Rules in Small States." Background paper, World Bank, Washington, DC.

Harding, Don, and Adrian Pagan. 2002. "Dissecting the Cycle: A Methodological Investigation." *Journal of Monetary Economics* 49 (2): 365–81.

Hnatkovska, Viktoria, and Friederike Koehler-Geib. 2018a. "Characterizing Business Cycles in Small Economies." Policy Research Working Paper 8527, World Bank, Washington, DC. http://documents.worldbank.org/curated/en/556931531406770669/pdf/WPS8527.pdf.

Hnatkovska, Viktoria, and Friederike Koehler-Geib. 2018b. "Sources of Volatility in Small Economies." Policy Research Working Paper 8526, World Bank, Washington, DC. http://documents.worldbank.org/curated/en/412821531405512576/pdf/WPS8526.pdf.

IMF (International Monetary Fund). Various years. World Economic Outlook. Washington, DC: IMF.

IMF (International Monetary Fund). Various years. International Financial Statistics database. Washington, DC: IMF.

Lederman, Daniel, and Justin Lesniak. 2017. "Open and Nimble: Finding Stable Growth in Small Economies." Regional Studies, Office of the Chief Economist for the Latin America and the Caribbean Region, World Bank, Washington, DC.

Male, Rachel. 2010. "Developing Country Business Cycles: Revisiting the Stylized Facts." Working Paper 664, School of Economics and Finance, Queen Mary University of London.

Neumeyer, Pablo A., and Fabrizio Perri. 2005. "Business Cycles in Emerging Economies: The Role of Interest Rates." *Journal of Monetary Economics* 52 (2): 345–80.

Raddatz, Claudio. 2007. "Are External Shocks Responsible for the Instability of Output in Low-Income Countries?" *Journal of Development Economics* 84 (1): 155–87.

Rand, John, and Finn Tarp. 2002. "Business Cycles in Developing Countries: Are They Different?" *World Development* 30 (12): 2071–88.

World Bank. Various years. World Development Indicators database. Washington, DC: World Bank.

2

The Impact of Fiscal Rules on Fiscal Performance

Over the last two decades, countries around the world have increasingly adopted fiscal rules. Debt rules and balance rules—among them budget balance rules rules—are the most common globally, but the use of expenditure rules has been rising in recent years. Meanwhile, revenue rules are the least common. The use of fiscal rules is also rising in smaller countries, including in Latin America and the Caribbean (LAC). Debt rules are the most common in smaller countries worldwide, including those in the LAC region. The popularity of balance rules in LAC peaked in the early 2000s but has since declined. Expenditure rules are less common but have been gaining space more recently. Their prevalence among LAC countries is comparable to that in other regions; however, while smaller countries worldwide have substantially increased their use of expenditure rules, smaller LAC countries have not. Many countries now combine multiple rules to achieve different objectives, but again, combined rules are less common in LAC and in smaller countries in general.

Compliance with fiscal rules among larger LAC countries is similar to compliance in other regions. But smaller LAC countries are less likely to comply with fiscal rules than both larger LAC countries and smaller countries in other regions. The study finds that adopting fiscal rules is associated with improvements in fiscal outcomes and that compliance with them strengthens this relationship. Balance rules and debt rules appear to be most effective in enhancing debt sustainability, while expenditure rules appear to reduce expenditure procyclicality, particularly when enforcement mechanisms are in place. However, these correlations are weaker in smaller LAC countries. The strength of each country's institutional and policy framework influences its compliance with fiscal rules, and the coverage of fiscal rules and their enforcement mechanisms have a particularly strong impact on compliance.

Introduction

Fiscal rules can strengthen macroeconomic management by reinforcing long-term debt sustainability and stabilizing short-term output fluctuations. However, the mere presence (without full compliance) of a fiscal rule does not guarantee that it will improve fiscal performance. Implementing effective fiscal rules requires a strong commitment to follow their provisions, an appropriate degree of flexibility to adapt to changing circumstances, adequate monitoring arrangements, and credible enforcement mechanisms. Failure to comply with fiscal rules not only reduces their effectiveness but also undermines the credibility and predictability of fiscal policy. The empirical literature reveals several factors that affect compliance with fiscal rules and influence their performance, including the overall quality of the fiscal framework, the type of rule or rules adopted, how they are enforced, and how easily they are altered (Auerbach 2014).

Empirical studies of the effectiveness of fiscal rules must overcome several analytical challenges. Fiscal rules and fiscal variables tend to display high persistence, thereby requiring the use of dynamic models to assess their impact on fiscal outcomes. Empirical assessments of the performance of fiscal rules also need to take into account the idiosyncrasies of countries regarding unobservable features in their fiscal structure, indicating the existence of individual country effects. In addition, evaluations of the effects of fiscal rules must also account for the endogeneity of these rules, including the potential for reverse causality between fiscal rules and fiscal performance. Last but not the least, assessments need to distinguish between the simple presence of fiscal rules and actual compliance with them. This chapter looks at these issues using a sample of 115 countries for the period 1985–2015.

This chapter examines both the adoption of fiscal rules and compliance with them, as well as their corresponding impact on fiscal outcomes. To analyze compliance, this study uses a newly created data set on actual compliance with fiscal rules using a global sample of 65 countries for the period 2000–15. In this context, the empirical analysis presented differentiates the presence of fiscal rules from compliance with them.[1] Moreover, the study also examines the underlying factors behind compliance or the lack of it in fiscal rules across countries.

The rest of the chapter is divided into five sections. The first section briefly presents a taxonomy of fiscal rules and ancillary mechanisms. The second section compares the adoption of fiscal rules in LAC and the rest of the world, placing additional focus on smaller countries. The third analyzes the extent to which fiscal rules are complied with and identifies the factors that affect compliance. The fourth section assesses the impact of fiscal rules on fiscal performance. The last section summarizes the findings of the analysis.

Taxonomy of Fiscal Rules

A fiscal rule is defined as a permanent constraint on fiscal policy through simple numerical limits on budgetary aggregates (see Kopits and Symansky 1998). A fiscal rule sets a numerical target over a long-lasting period to guide fiscal policy, specifies a summary operational fiscal indicator to which it is applicable, and is simple so that it can be readily operationalized, communicated to the public, and monitored.

Depending on the budgetary aggregate that they aim to regulate, fiscal rules can be grouped into four main types (figure 2.1):

- *Balance rules* focus generally on government fiscal balances[2]. There are two main types of balance rules:

    a. *Budget balance rules* define numerical targets for actual government fiscal balances, normally in terms of gross domestic product (GDP). Budget balance rules have direct and strong links with debt sustainability objectives, as their numerical targets directly affect debt dynamics and are defined to ensure that the debt-to-GDP ratio converges with a targeted debt level.

    b. *Structural balance rules* target the estimated budget balance that would result if output were at its long-term potential and filter out one-time fiscal transactions that do not affect the intertemporal fiscal position of

FIGURE 2.1: **A Basic Taxonomy of Fiscal Rules**

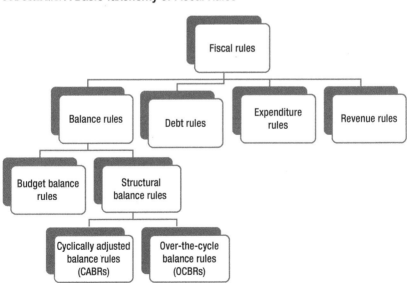

Source: Based on Commonwealth Secretariat and World Bank 2000.

the government (for example, privatizations, extraordinary spending related to policy changes such as social security and civil service reforms). In countries where commodity export proceeds are relevant, this type of rule takes into account the effect of commodity price cycles on fiscal balances.[3]

- *Debt rules* set numerical limits for public debt typically as a percentage of GDP. Because of their explicit link to debt stocks, debt rules tend to be the most direct tool for ensuring that annual budget balances are consistent with sustainable debt levels. When actual debt levels are far from the targets, debt rules do not provide clear operational guidance for the definition of annual budget targets.

- *Expenditure rules* set limits on the level or growth rate of government spending. Containing the size of government is a key function of expenditure rules. As they establish fixed targets for the level or growth of government expenditures, expenditure rules also reduce spending procyclicality and support output stabilization.

- *Revenue rules* set floors or ceilings on government revenue. They can help to improve revenue collection or prevent an excessive tax burden, but they do not ensure debt sustainability. In addition, revenue rules that set revenue floors or ceilings tend to introduce procyclicality, as they prevent the operation of automatic stabilizers on the revenue side of the budget. Nonetheless, by defining the use of windfall or higher-than-expected revenues, some revenue rules can support debt sustainability and reduce procyclical spending.

Escape clauses are a key tool for mitigating the trade-off between a government's commitment to the adoption of fiscal rules and its need for flexibility to address extraordinary events. Both time-inconsistency problems and the fact that fiscal rules can never be fully contingent inevitably create situations in which strict compliance with the rule may be fiscally unfeasible and costly and economically suboptimal. Instead of circumventing the rule, well-defined escape clauses embedded in the rule can provide flexibility without affecting the credibility, enforceability, and predictability of the rule.

Sovereign wealth funds are complementary instruments that can enhance the functioning of both budget balance and structural balance rules. Sovereign wealth funds can facilitate fiscal stabilization, where the primary objective is to insulate the budget and the economy against commodity price swings and the effects of the economic cycle. In case of an economic slowdown when borrowing conditions are adverse, the government can use assets in a stabilization fund without having to access the markets, which has a favorable effect on interest rates for both public and private sector borrowing, mitigating the effects of the cycle. Moreover, they can safeguard fiscal resources for long-term objectives, such as preparing for an aging population or facilitating intergenerational transfers, by converting nonrenewable assets into a more diversified portfolio. Sovereign wealth funds also help to mitigate the effects of Dutch disease or meet long-term liabilities.

The institutional framework surrounding the functioning of fiscal rules can be strengthened by the establishment of fiscal councils. Fiscal councils reinforce the commitment of fiscal authorities because they raise the reputational and political costs of deviations to the rule by monitoring compliance and providing independent technical advice to the government on the macrofiscal projections used to set targets embedded in the rules. Fiscal councils also perform other functions that are not related to the functioning of fiscal rules, such as evaluating the fiscal impact of policy decisions or government programs and reforms and assessing medium-term fiscal sustainability.

Presence of Fiscal Rules

In recent decades, the number of countries with fiscal rules has increased steadily, rising from 7 in 1990 to 49 in 2000 and reaching 92 in 2015. Of these, 48 countries with fiscal rules had populations above the global median set in this study, while 44 had populations below the median. In 2015, 17 of the 33 LAC countries had adopted at least one fiscal rule (figure 2.2). These included 11 countries with national fiscal rules as well as the 6 member states of the Eastern Caribbean Currency Union (ECCU), which employs supranational fiscal rules.[4]

Fiscal rules are as common in smaller LAC countries as they are in smaller countries in the rest of the world and in large LAC countries. The number of smaller LAC countries adopting fiscal rules has had a significant bump-up due to the existence of the supranational rule adopted by the ECCU, which incorporates six countries.

FIGURE 2.2: **Number of Fiscal Rules, by Country Size and Region, 1985–2015**

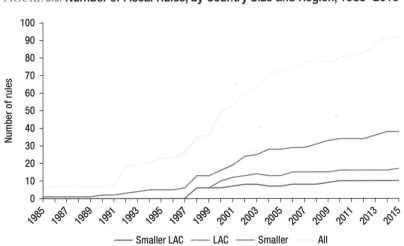

Source: Calculations based on data from the Fiscal Rules Dataset (IMF 2015).

Globally, about half of all large countries have adopted fiscal rules compared with 45 percent of smaller ones. At 52 percent, the share of LAC countries with fiscal rules is similar to the global average, but well below the 66 percent average for high-income countries and the 66 percent average for Europe and Central Asia, the region with the most rules (figure 2.3).

Globally, debt rules and balance rules are the most common. Balance rules include both budget balance rules and structural balance rules, with budget balance rules being the overwhelming majority within this group of rules.[5] In 2015 more than 70 debt and balance rules were in place in countries around the world. Expenditure rules are less common, but their number has risen sharply in recent years, from 23 in 2011 to 45 in 2015 (figure 2.4). The number of expenditure rules adopted by smaller countries tripled over the period, but smaller LAC countries only began adopting them in 2015. Finally, combinations of rules have become more common over time. More than 70 countries now employ a combination of debt and balance rules, debt and expenditure rules, or balance and expenditure rules (Bova et al. 2015; Skrok et al. 2017).

FIGURE 2.3: **Percent of Countries with Fiscal Rules, by Country Size and Region, 2015**

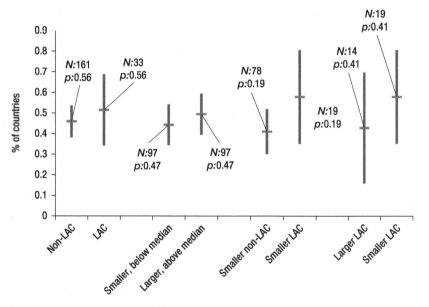

Source: Calculations based on data from the Fiscal Rules Dataset (IMF 2015).
Note: Figure shows the share of countries with any type of fiscal rule in each country group. Vertical lines = 95 percent confidence interval for the sample average. Horizontal lines = sample averages. N = number of observations in each category. p = p-values for the test that the average of a given indicator for each subgroup is equal to the average outside the group. The figure makes four comparisons: (a) between non-LAC and LAC countries; (b) between smaller and larger countries; (c) between smaller non-LAC and LAC countries; and (d) between larger and smaller LAC countries.

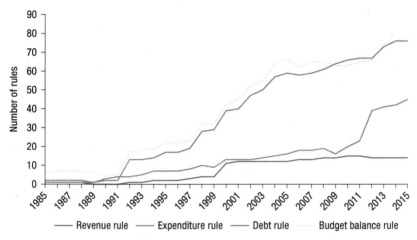

FIGURE 2.4: **Number of Fiscal Rules, by Type of Rule, 1985–2015**

—— Revenue rule   —— Expenditure rule   —— Debt rule   Budget balance rule

Source: Calculations based on data from the Fiscal Rules Dataset (IMF 2015).

Debt rules are the most common type of fiscal rule in smaller countries world-wide, LAC countries, and smaller LAC countries. More than 30 percent of smaller countries worldwide use a debt rule (figure 2.5). While debt rules are also the most popular type of fiscal rule in the LAC region, LAC countries tend to use fewer debt and balance rules than countries in other regions. However, within the LAC region, smaller countries use more debt and balance rules than larger countries. Again, the number of smaller LAC countries with a debt rule is bumped up by the supranational debt ceiling adopted by ECCU member countries. The popularity of balance rules in LAC peaked in the early 2000s but has since declined. The use of expenditure rules is comparable in LAC countries and other regions. Expenditure rules are very popular among large LAC countries, but less so in smaller LAC countries.

Combining rules has become very common worldwide, but less so among smaller countries and countries in the LAC region. Smaller countries are somewhat less likely than large countries to use a combination of rules. Smaller countries that combine rules most often use a debt rule and a budget balance rule, although combining a debt rule with an expenditure rule is becoming more common. Combined rules are less common in LAC than in other regions. About 12 percent of LAC countries use the combination of debt rule and balance rule, compared to 37 percent of non-LAC countries (figure 2.6). While smaller LAC countries use this combination more than large LAC countries, they use it less than smaller countries in other regions. The combination of expenditure rules with debt or balance rules is also less common in LAC, especially in smaller LAC countries. Indeed, in 2015 only one smaller LAC country combined an expenditure rule with a debt rule and just two smaller LAC countries

FIGURE 2.5: Use of Fiscal Rules, by Type of Rule, Region, and Country Size, 2015

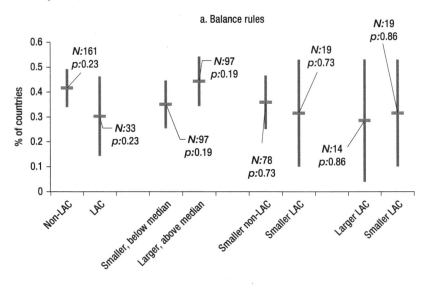

a. Balance rules

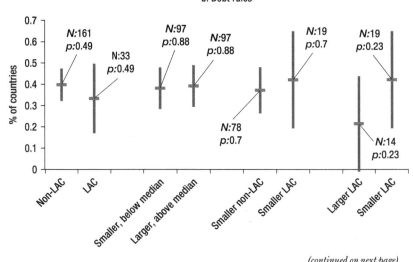

b. Debt rules

(continued on next page)

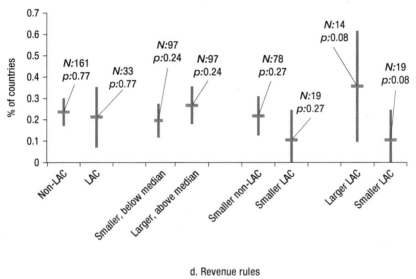

c. Expenditure rules

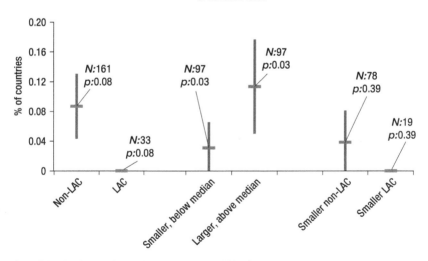

d. Revenue rules

Source: Calculations based on data from the Fiscal Rules Dataset (IMF 2015).

Note: Figure shows the number of countries using each type of rule as a share of all countries in each region and size group. Vertical lines = the 95 percent confidence interval for the sample average. Horizontal lines = sample averages. N = number of observations in each category. p = p-values for the test that the average of a given indicator for each subgroup is equal to the average outside the group. Panels a., b., and c. make four comparisons: (a) between non-LAC and LAC countries; (b) between smaller and larger countries; (c) between smaller non-LAC and LAC countries; and (d) between larger and smaller LAC countries. Panel d. makes three comparisons: (a) between non-LAC and LAC countries; (b) between smaller and larger countries; and (c) between smaller non-LAC and LAC countries.

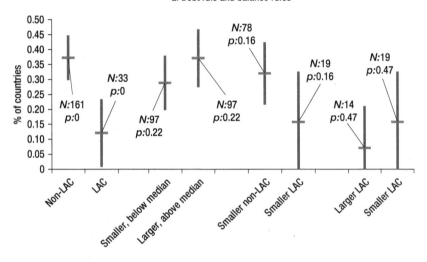

a. Debt rule and balance rules

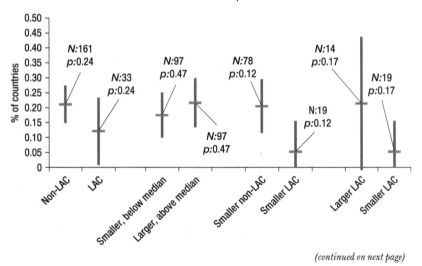

b. Debt rule and expenditure rules

(continued on next page)

c. Balance rule and expenditure rule

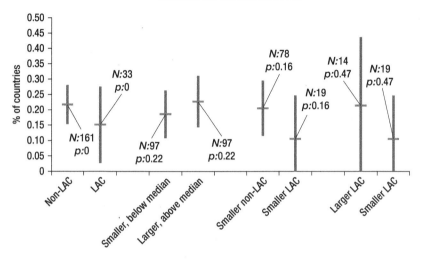

Source: Calculations based on data from the Fiscal Rules Dataset (IMF 2015).
Note: Figure shows the number of countries with specific rule combinations as a share of all countries in each region and size group. Vertical lines = 95 percent confidence interval for the sample average. Horizontal lines = sample averages. N = number of observations in each category; p = p-values for the test that the average of a given indicator for each subgroup is equal to the average outside the group. The figure makes four comparisons: (a) between non-LAC and LAC countries; (b) between smaller and larger countries; (c) between smaller non-LAC and LAC countries; and (d) between larger and smaller LAC countries.

combined an expenditure rule with a budget balance rule. Large LAC countries are more likely to use combinations of an expenditure rule with a debt rule or a budget balance rule than any other comparison group presented in figure 2.6 (all non-LAC countries, smaller and large countries worldwide, smaller non-LAC and smaller LAC countries).

Compliance with Fiscal Rules and Contributing Factors

This study has built a data set on actual compliance with fiscal rules using a global sample of 65 countries for the period 2000–15.[6] The analysis of compliance presented in this section is based on two approaches. The first compares the statutory provisions of each fiscal rule with the respective country's targeted fiscal indicators, as estimated by World Bank country economists. The second compares the statutory provisions of each fiscal rule with the fiscal outcomes and policy actions reported in all available International Monetary Fund (IMF) Article IV consultation staff reports, World Bank staff reports, Organisation for Economic Co-operation and Development (OECD) and European Commission reports, and publicly accessible research papers. The new data set includes 10 LAC countries and 55 countries in other regions. Of all countries in the data set, 29 have populations below the global median, and 36 have populations above the median set in this study.[7]

Adopting a fiscal rule does not ensure that the government will comply with it. Compliance reflects each government's ability and commitment to remain within the statutory parameters established by its fiscal rule or rules. An analysis of average global compliance rates over 2000–15 reveals a significant gap between the presence of fiscal rules and actual compliance, with compliance varying substantially from country to country and by type of rule.

Over the 2000–15 period, debt rules had the highest compliance rates, balance rules had the lowest, and the compliance rates of expenditure rules rose. As debt rules apply a ceiling to a variable stock of debt rather than to a flow of debt and these ceilings can be set well above actual debt levels, they tend to be easier to comply with than other types of rules. The relatively simple design of debt rules also facilitates monitoring and enforcement. Most countries are able to comply with them unless they face very strong macroeconomic shocks that substantially affect their debt-to-GDP ratios or they have continuous budget deficits that they are unable to stabilize before the debt limit is reached. By contrast, compliance with balance rules is the lowest of the three types of rules analyzed because balance rules establish targets that must be met annually, which means that macroeconomic shocks have a more immediate effect on compliance. As structural balance rules or cyclically adjusted rules are better able to cope with growth shocks, they may have somewhat higher compliance rates.

Compliance with debt rules and balance rules dropped in the aftermath of the global financial crisis, while compliance with expenditure rules increased. The extensive, continuous fiscal deterioration that followed the crisis negatively affected compliance rates for balance rules and, to a lesser extent, for debt rules. Meanwhile, compliance with expenditure rules rose and now exceeds the rate for both debt and balance rules (figure 2.7).

Compliance rates among smaller LAC countries are significantly below those of both large LAC countries and smaller countries worldwide. Compliance among smaller countries worldwide tracks the overall pattern of compliance for all countries. While compliance improved in LAC overall, the same is not true for compliance among smaller LAC countries (figure 2.8). Compliance rates in smaller countries worldwide and LAC countries are similar to those of large countries and the rest of the world. However, smaller LAC countries have lower compliance rates than both other small countries in the world and large countries in LAC (Skrok et al. 2017).

Smaller LAC countries have lower compliance rates for balance rules and debt rules than smaller countries worldwide and large LAC countries. Globally, smaller and large countries have similar compliance rates for balance rules and debt rules. Compliance with both balance rules and debt rules is higher in LAC than in other

FIGURE 2.7: **Average Compliance with Fiscal Rules, by Type of Rule and before and after the Global Financial Crisis, 2000–15**

a. Average compliance with all fiscal rules

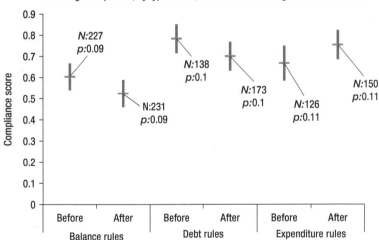

b. Average compliance, by type of rule, before and after the global financial crisis

Sources: Calculations based on World Bank data on compliance with fiscal rules; Skrok et al. 2017.

Note: In panel b, 1 = full compliance, and 0 = noncompliance. Thus a score of 0.9 = a given country group complied with its fiscal rules in 90 percent of observations over the period. Vertical lines = 95 percent confidence interval for the sample average. Horizontal lines = sample averages. N = the number of observations in each category. p = p-values for this test.

Compliance with Fiscal Rules, by Country Size and Region, 2000–15

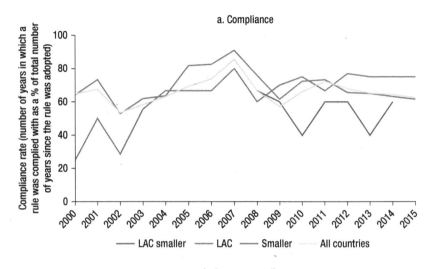

a. Compliance

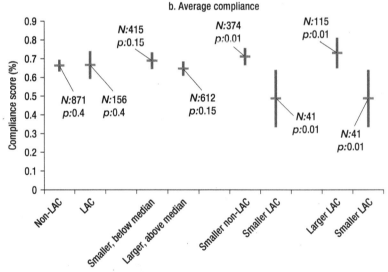

b. Average compliance

Sources: Calculations based on World Bank data on compliance with fiscal rules; Skrok et al. 2017.

Note: In panel b, 1 = full compliance. 0 = noncompliance. Thus a score of 0.9 implies that a given country group complied with its fiscal rules in 90 percent of observations over the period. Vertical = 95 percent confidence interval for the sample average. Horizontal lines = sample averages. *N* = number of observations in each category. *p* = *p*-values for the test that the average of a given indicator for each subgroup is equal to the average outside the group. Panel b makes four comparisons: (a) between non-LAC and LAC countries; (b) between smaller and larger countries; (c) between smaller non-LAC and LAC countries; and (d) between larger and smaller LAC countries.

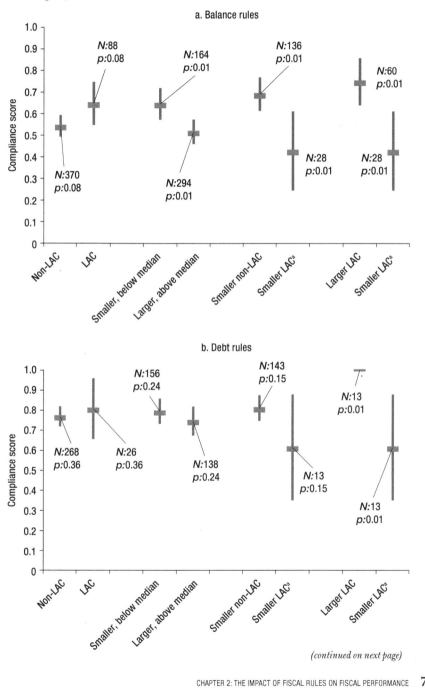

FIGURE 2.9: Compliance with Fiscal Rules, by Type of Rule, Country Size, and Region, 2000–15

(continued on next page)

c. Expenditure rules

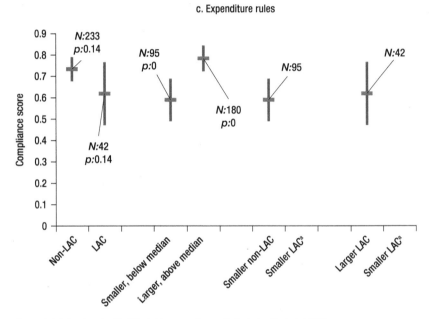

Sources: Calculations based on World Bank data on compliance with fiscal rules; Skrok et al. 2017.
Note: Vertical lines = 95 percent confidence interval for the sample average. Horizontal lines = sample averages. *N* = number of observations in each category. *p* = *p*-values for the test that the average of a given indicator for each subgroup is equal to the average outside the group. The figure makes four comparisons: (a) between non-LAC and LAC countries; (b) between smaller and larger countries; (c) between smaller non-LAC and LAC countries; and (d) between larger and smaller LAC countries.
a. No observations.

regions, but it is relatively low in smaller LAC countries. Smaller LAC countries are more likely to comply with debt rules than with other types of rules, but their average compliance with debt rules, at 62 percent, is well below the average rate, at 81 percent, for smaller countries worldwide and for large LAC countries that fully comply with debt rules (figure 2.9).

Globally, compliance with expenditure rules has improved significantly since the global financial crisis, but compliance rates remain lowest among smaller countries. Among large countries, compliance with expenditure rules is higher than it is for other fiscal rules, at 78 percent. Compliance with expenditure rules is lower for LAC countries than for non-LAC countries. Smaller LAC countries have only recently begun adopting expenditure rules, and compliance rates for this group of countries are not yet available (Cordes et al. 2015).

Compliance with fiscal rules is influenced by the overall fiscal framework. To assess the factors behind compliance, it is important to situate fiscal rules within the overall fiscal framework in force in a country. The fiscal framework is the set of laws, regulations, institutions, and instruments that shape fiscal policies and support their implementation. More specifically, the fiscal framework surrounding fiscal rules typically consists of four main dimensions: (a) the legal basis of the fiscal rule, its technical design, escape clauses, and correction and enforcement mechanisms; (b) the presence of fiscal councils that monitor compliance with the rule and normally provide technical advice to the government on preparing macrofiscal projections to instrument the rule (box 2.1); (c) the budgetary and public financial management systems and procedural arrangements, including the norms for preparing and executing the government budget, use of a medium-term fiscal framework underpinning preparation of the budget, fiscal accounting system, and coverage of public accounts; and (d) sovereign wealth funds or stabilization funds that interact with the fiscal rules and are expected to strengthen their functioning (figure 2.10).

BOX 2.1: Fiscal Councils

Fiscal councils reinforce the commitment of fiscal authorities to fiscal rules because they increase the costs of their noncompliance. Fiscal councils are permanent entities with the mandate to evaluate publicly and independently fiscal policy and its performance with respect to the objectives of sustainability of public finances and macroeconomic stabilization, issuing nonbinding opinions through reports and special studies. A fiscal council's independence enhances the credibility of the overall institutional framework where fiscal rules operate.

Fiscal councils have diverse functions, depending on whether their mandates are broadly defined or refer specifically to fiscal rules. The most common functions of fiscal councils are to (a) monitor the implementation of fiscal rules; (b) provide independent technical advice to the government on macrofiscal projections, including medium-term fiscal strategies; (c) evaluate the long-term fiscal sustainability of public finances, (d) estimate the cost of new public policy initiatives; and (e) propose policy options to address fiscal policy issues. In any case, the functions of a fiscal council must be compatible with its mandate and clearly defined in the legal framework.

The effectiveness of a fiscal council depends on the following dimensions:

- *Legal or statutory basis (the higher level, the better).* Established through acts, by-laws, regulations, and decrees
- *Institutional setup.* An independent council or part of the ministry of finance or the legislature

(continued on next page)

- *Structure.* A council of well-known specialists and a permanent technical secretariat with budget autonomy, which is key for its proper functioning
- *Appointment, tenure, and termination procedures for members of the council*
- *Scope of coverage.* Central government, general government (including subnational governments), and nonfinancial public sector
- *Mandate.* Wide, with several functions, or specific to the monitoring of compliance with the fiscal rule
- *Communication.* Direct channels of communication with the ministry of finance and other government agencies and also with the legislative power as well as communication with the public at large through the regular publication of reports.

Fiscal councils that have strong legal basis, are more autonomous, have members with fixed terms, are adequately resourced and financed, have well-defined mandates, and are influential in the public debate on fiscal policy can be more effective in enhancing the functioning of fiscal rules and overall fiscal policy management.

In different shapes and forms and with different levels of success, several LAC countries have established fiscal councils, including The Bahamas (2017), Brazil (2016), Chile (2013, modified in 2019), Colombia (2012), Grenada (2017), Guyana (2019), Mexico (1998), Panama (2018), Paraguay (2016), and Peru (2016). These councils are heterogeneous in terms of the dimensions mentioned above. Fiscal councils in Chile and Colombia have very specific mandates related to the preparation of macroeconomic projections for defining the targets of fiscal rules. The fiscal council in Grenada has a specific mandate related to monitoring the government's compliance with fiscal rules, while the fiscal council in Guyana has the mandate to monitor and assess compliance with the Natural Resource Fund Act and management of its sovereign wealth fund and to provide an independent assessment of the management and use of the resources of the fund. Other fiscal councils in the region have broader mandates. Fiscal councils in Chile and Paraguay are part of the structure of the ministry of finance, while those in Brazil and Mexico are part of congress (under different legal figures). Fiscal councils in Colombia, Guyana, and Peru have autonomous structures. Fiscal councils in Brazil and Peru communicate actively with the public through regular reports and special studies, while fiscal councils in Chile[a] and Paraguay communicate internally and play advisory roles within the ministry of finance.[b]

a. In 2019 Chile's fiscal council was strengthened and given more autonomy.

b. More detailed information and classification of fiscal councils can be found in the International Monetary Fund's Fiscal Council Dataset, available at imf.org/external/np/fad/council.

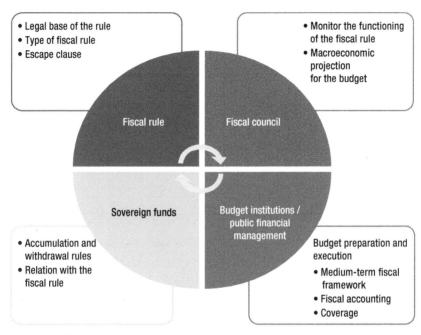

FIGURE 2.10: **Fiscal Rules and the Overall Fiscal Framework**

- Legal base of the rule
- Type of fiscal rule
- Escape clause

- Monitor the functioning of the fiscal rule
- Macroeconomic projection for the budget

Fiscal rule

Fiscal council

Sovereign funds

Budget institutions / public financial management

- Accumulation and withdrawal rules
- Relation with the fiscal rule

Budget preparation and execution
- Medium-term fiscal framework
- Fiscal accounting
- Coverage

Source: World Bank.

The empirical analysis undertaken for this study indicates that a strong institutional and fiscal policy framework favors compliance with fiscal rules. A Fiscal Rule Strength Index (FRSI) was used to measure the institutional framework of fiscal rules.[8] The FRSI reflects five dimensions of rule strength: (1) statutory basis of the rule, (2) monitoring arrangements, (3) formal enforcement mechanisms, (4) coverage of the fiscal accounts to which the rule is applied, and (5) definition of escape clauses.

Countries with high FRSI scores are more likely to comply with their fiscal rules. Countries in compliance with a balance rule have an average FRSI score of 0.62, while countries not in compliance have an average score of 0.56 (figure 2.11). Similarly, the average FRSI score for countries in compliance with a debt rule is 0.56, compared with an average score for noncompliant countries of 0.44. Compliance with expenditure rules is also positively associated with the FRSI score. While these results suggest that the features of national institutional and policy frameworks influence compliance, correlation does not necessarily imply causation. For example, countries with high FSRI scores may be more likely to comply with fiscal rules not because the former causes the latter, but because both factors reflect the underlying sophistication, efficacy, and credibility of their fiscal policies.

FIGURE 2.11: **Fiscal Rule Strength Index (FRSI), by Type of Rule and Compliance, 1985–2013**

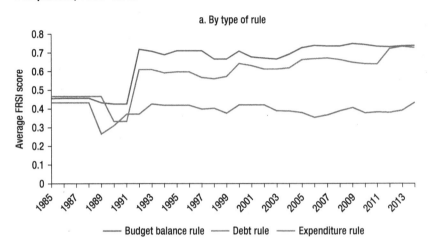

a. By type of rule

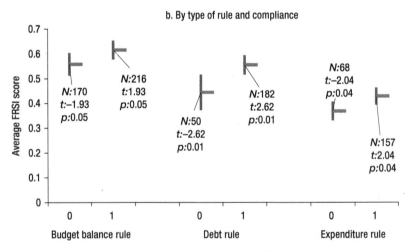

b. By type of rule and compliance

Sources: Calculations based on World Bank data on compliance with fiscal rules; Skrok et al. 2017.
Note: In panel b, vertical lines = 95 percent confidence interval for the sample average. Horizontal lines = sample averages. *N* = number of observations in each category. *t* = *t*-statistics for the test that the average of a given indicator for each subgroup is equal to the average outside the group. *p* = *p*-values for this test. 0 = no compliance, 1 = compliance.

Regression analysis shows that the presence of enforcement mechanisms and the broad coverage of fiscal rules are both associated with higher compliance rates. This correlation is shown by a simple panel logit model that includes various components of the FRSI as well as four additional explanatory variables: the output gap, logged GDP per capita, logged population, and a dummy representing the drivers of compliance. The results indicate that the broader the coverage of government accounts included in balance and debt rules, the higher the compliance rate (Bova et al. 2015). Formal enforcement procedures—such as automatic correction mechanisms, predetermined consequences for noncompliance, and clearly defined authority to take corrective action—appear to increase compliance. Neither a rule's monitoring mechanism nor its legal basis appears to explain differences in compliance rates (Skrok et al. 2017).

Performance of Fiscal Rules

This section assesses the performance of fiscal rules in terms of their ability to improve fiscal balances, reduce debt levels, control the growth of spending, and attenuate the cyclicality of fiscal policy. While the existing evidence on the effectiveness of fiscal rules in improving fiscal performance is still is mixed and focuses on developed countries (most of them European Union countries), empirical studies have generally found that fiscal rules enhance fiscal discipline. Both cross-country analyses and country-specific empirical studies have underscored the efficacy of numeric rules in improving fiscal discipline (Debrun 2008, 2013; European Commission 2009; Fall et al. 2015; Iara and Wolff 2011; Marneffe et al. 2011). Some countries have successfully used fiscal rules to align macrofiscal variables with national policy goals, but compliance has been inconsistent (Heinemann, Moessinger, and Yeter 2016; Wyplosz 2013). Indeed, the evidence presented in these studies suggests that fiscal rules tend to have a greater impact on debt sustainability when combined with supportive legal and institutional arrangements, such as a fiscal council and a medium-term budget framework (Nerlich and Reuter 2013).

While the design of and compliance with rules are important, structural factors also influence the effectiveness of fiscal rules. Multiple factors affect fiscal outcomes that are beyond the control of policy makers, such as the initial stock of public debt, the country's level of economic development, the stability of the inflation rate, the volatility of the terms of trade, the extent of the country's integration with global financial markets, its endowment of natural resources, its governance quality and political stability, and the law enforcement and monitoring arrangements underpinning the fiscal rule. All of these factors can affect the relationship between fiscal rules and fiscal performance.[9]

Most studies of fiscal rules and fiscal performance focus on advanced economies, and those studies that use a global sample often do not distinguish between large and smaller countries, between developed and developing countries, or between countries in different geographic regions. In addition, nearly all cross-country studies regard the *presence* of fiscal rules as the independent variable, without accounting for the extent to which governments actually comply with those rules. Complementing a smaller but growing body of empirical evidence on the impact of fiscal rules, the findings of the assessment undertaken for this report show that the impact of fiscal rules on fiscal performance depends on compliance and that country size has a meaningful influence on compliance (Schmidt-Hebbel and Soto 2018). The analysis below focuses on three aspects—the cyclicality of fiscal policy, fiscal balances, and the reaction of primary balances to changes in debt levels—and examines how type of rule, country size, and region (LAC/non-LAC) influence the extent to which fiscal rules affect these dimensions.

Impact on the Cyclicality of Fiscal Policy

Adopting an expenditure rule tends to reduce expenditure procyclicality, and this effect is stronger when it is combined with a fiscal council and when it interacts with a sovereign wealth fund, while the effectiveness of expenditure rules in reducing spending procyclicality is weaker in smaller countries.[10] Adopting any of the three major fiscal rules—a balance rule, a debt rule, or an expenditure rule—can help to stabilize public spending; however, among a global sample of countries, only the impact of an expenditure rule is statistically significant (figure 2.12, panel a). The estimated coefficient suggests that implementing an expenditure rule can reduce expenditure procyclicality by as much as 40 percent. Moreover, the presence of a fiscal council or a sovereign wealth fund enhances the stabilizing effect of expenditure rules. An important aspect of a sovereign wealth fund complementing the functioning of fiscal rules is that, as such funds help to attenuate the volatility of government revenues, they indirectly favor the stabilization of government expenditures. The positive effect of expenditure rules on fiscal procyclicality is magnified by population, meaning that the ability of expenditure rules to reduce procyclicality is weaker but still significant in smaller countries.

The assessment of the effects of fiscal rules on fiscal balances[11] confirms that expenditure rules are effective in reducing procyclicality in LAC countries. Worldwide, budget balance rules, expenditure rules, and debt rules reduce procyclicality (have a positive effect on fiscal balances), but this relation is statistically insignificant (figure 2.12, panel b). In contrast, in LAC the effect of expenditure rules on fiscal balances is positive, higher, and significant, which confirms that expenditure rules are more effective in reducing procyclicality. Debt rules tend to reduce procyclicality in LAC, too, but their effect remains insignificant. Results also show that budget balance rules make fiscal policy more procyclical in LAC countries. Leaving aside the issue of statistical significance, results clearly show that expenditure rules are more effective in reducing the procyclicality of fiscal balances than debt rules and balance rules (which in fact favor procyclicality) and

FIGURE 2.12: **Impact of Fiscal Rules on 10-Year Procyclicality, by Type of Rule and Country Characteristics**

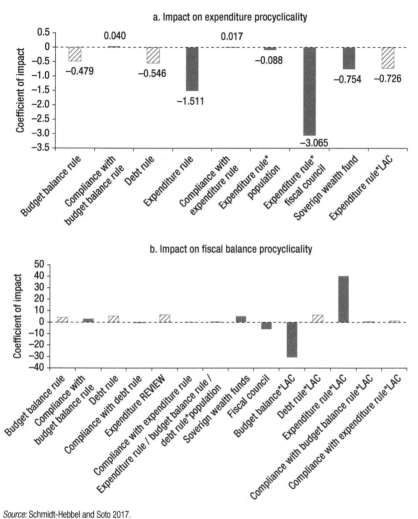

a. Impact on expenditure procyclicality

0.040   0.017   −0.479   −0.546   −1.511   −0.088   −3.065   −0.754   −0.726

b. Impact on fiscal balance procyclicality

Source: Schmidt-Hebbel and Soto 2017.

Note: In panel a, a negative estimated coefficient indicates that rules are effective in reducing expenditure procyclicality. In panel b, a positive estimated coefficient indicates that rules are effective in improving fiscal discipline (increase budget balance). In both panels, the solid fill indicates statistical significance.

that sovereign wealth funds enhance the stabilizing role of expenditure rules. Overall, economic size does not seem to have an impact on the effectiveness of fiscal rules, except for budget balance rules, which display a negative estimate, implying that in small economies this type of rule exacerbates the procyclicality of the fiscal balance.

Impact on Short-Term Sustainability: Effects on Fiscal Balances and Debt

While globally, balance rules, debt rules, and expenditure rules improve fiscal balances, their effectiveness in supporting fiscal sustainability is dubious in LAC countries and smaller economies. Worldwide, the positive effects of the three types of rules on the fiscal balance are significant, with debt rules having stronger effects on fiscal balances. While regional differences are not statistically significant, results show that the effectiveness of fiscal rules is lower in the LAC region. An interesting finding is that budget balance rules have the expected positive result of improving the fiscal balance globally, but they have the opposite effect in LAC countries, although the results are not significant. One possible explanation is that, before adopting rules, LAC countries had stricter fiscal balance targets and that, while reinforcing the institutional and longer term commitment with fiscal discipline, the adoption of budget balance rules implied the definition of less restrictive targets. Results also suggest that budget balance rules and expenditure rules are less effective in smaller countries and that debt rules tend to have negative effects on fiscal balances.

Budget balance, debt, and expenditure rules are not significantly associated with lower debt levels unless they are accompanied by a fiscal council (figure 2.13). Merely having a rule in place is not tantamount to debt control. Worldwide, countries

FIGURE 2.13: **Impact of Fiscal Rules on Public Debt Levels, by Type of Rule and Country Characteristics**

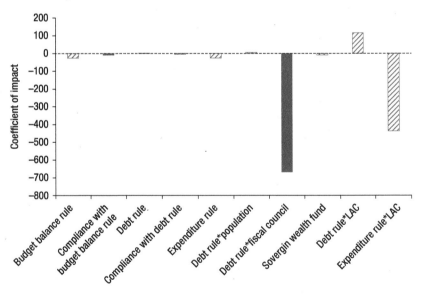

Source: Schmidt-Hebbel and Soto 2018.
Note: A negative estimated coefficient indicates that rules are effective in reducing the debt level. The solid fill indicates statistical significance.

adopting fiscal rules exhibit lower debt levels, but this result is not statistically significant. This finding applies to the global sample, the LAC region, and small economies, except for budget balance rules, which have a positive and significant effect on indebtedness in both LAC and smaller countries. Fiscal councils seem to enhance the effectiveness of both balance and debt rules in controlling debt levels.

Impact on Medium-Term Debt Sustainability

Balance rules and debt rules are associated with improved long term debt sustainability, as they tend to increase the responsiveness of the primary balance to changes in the debt stock; in the case of balance rules, compliance enhances their impact.[12] These rules increase the sensitivity of the primary balance by 0.6–0.8 percentage point of GDP for each 10-percentage-point increase in the debt stock. Compliance with balance rules greatly intensifies this effect (figure 2.14). Adopting a debt rule also increases the responsiveness of the primary balance to changes in the debt stock, but compliance with the debt rule does not enhance its impact. This may reflect the high

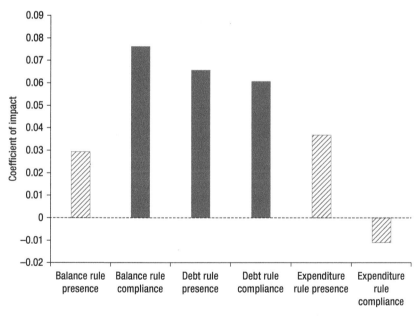

FIGURE 2.14: **Impact of Fiscal Rules on the Responsiveness of the Primary Balance to Changes in the Stock of Debt, by Type of Rule**

Sources: Calculations based on World Bank data on compliance with fiscal rules; Skrok et al. 2017.
Note: A positive coefficient indicates that the fiscal rule strengthens the responsiveness of the primary balance to an increase in the debt stock. The solid fill denotes statistical significance.

rate of compliance with debt rules among countries in the sample group and the fact that when actual debt levels are far from their target levels, debt rules do not require improvements in the primary balance in the short run. Finally, expenditure rules have no statistically significant impact on debt sustainability. This result is not surprising, as expenditure rules influence only one side of the budget equation and are not expected to unequivocally promote improvements in fiscal balances.

Among large countries, fiscal rules appear to have a positive and statistically significant impact on debt sustainability. This is especially true for large countries that comply with balance rules. Although fiscal rules have a generally positive impact on the responsiveness of the primary surplus in smaller countries, this finding is only statistically robust among smaller countries that comply with debt rules. In large countries, compliance tends to intensify the impact of fiscal rules on debt sustainability, and compliance with balance rules has the greatest positive effect (figure 2.15). In smaller countries, adopting fiscal rules has no statistically significant impact on long term debt sustainability, but complying with debt rules substantially improves debt sustainability.

FIGURE 2.15: Impact of Fiscal Rules on the Responsiveness of the Primary Balance to Changes in the Debt Stock, by Type of Rule and Country Size

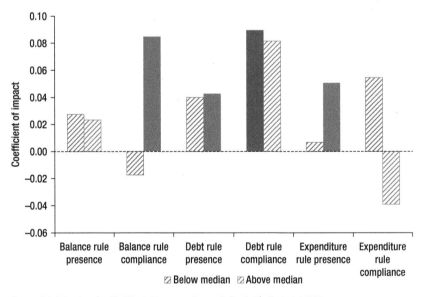

Sources: Calculations based on World Bank data on compliance with fiscal rules; Skrok et al. 2017.
Note: A positive coefficient indicates that the fiscal rule strengthens the responsiveness of the primary balance to an increase in the debt stock. The solid fill denotes statistical significance.

Combining rules intensifies their positive impact on debt sustainability. Due to the increased prevalence of combined fiscal rules after the global financial crisis of 2008–09, this analysis compares the impact of various combinations of rules in the periods before and after the crisis. The results show that adopting a combination of fiscal rules—especially a combination of debt and expenditure rules or debt and balance rules—is associated with more improvement in debt sustainability than adopting any single rule. These combinations increase the responsiveness of the primary balance to changes in the debt stock by 1.5–1.8 percentage points of GDP for each 10-percentage-point increase in the debt stock, roughly twice the impact of any singe rule (figure 2.16).

Overall, results show that actual compliance reinforces fiscal sustainability. As mentioned, globally, the presence of any type of fiscal rule has a positive but, in some cases, statistically insignificant effect on fiscal balances, debt stock, and primary balances. However, this effect becomes significant among countries that comply with balance rules. Moreover, in LAC, the presence of a balance rule is associated with lower fiscal balances, but compliance with the rule is associated with a slight improvement in fiscal balances, although this result is not statistically significant in all of the specifications (table 2.1).

FIGURE 2.16: **Impact of Fiscal Rules on the Responsiveness of the Primary Balance to Changes in the Stock of Debt, by Combinations of Rules**

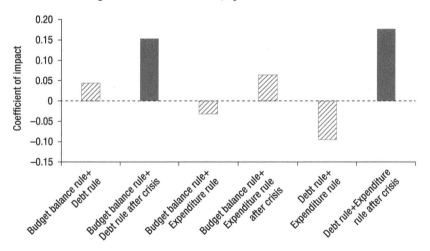

Sources: Calculations based on World Bank data on compliance with fiscal rules; Skrok et al. 2017.
Note: A positive coefficient indicates that the fiscal rule strengthens the responsiveness of the primary balance to an increase in the debt stock. The solid fill denotes statistical significance.

TABLE 2.1: **Effects of Fiscal Rules: Summary of Findings**

Effect	Balance rules	Debt rules	Expenditure rules
Procyclicality (government expenditures)			
Is procyclicality reduced?	No	No	Yes
Is procyclicality reduced in smaller countries?	No	No	Yes, but less
Is procyclicality reduced in LAC countries?	No	No	Yes, and strongly
Do fiscal councils help to reduce procyclicality?	No	No	Yes
Do sovereign wealth funds help to reduce procyclicality?	No	No	Yes
Procyclicality (fiscal balance)			
Is procyclicality reduced?	Yes, but not significantly	Yes, but not significantly	Yes, but not significantly
Is procyclicality reduced in smaller countries?	No, exacerbates	No	No
Is procyclicality reduced in LAC countries?	Yes, significantly	Yes, significantly	Yes, significantly
Do fiscal councils help to reduce procyclicality?	No	No	No
Do sovereign wealth funds help to reduce procyclicality?	No	No	No
Short-term fiscal sustainability (fiscal balance)			
Do fiscal balances improve?	Yes	Yes	Yes
Do fiscal balances improve in smaller countries?	Yes, but weakly	Yes, but weakly	Yes, but weakly
Do fiscal balances improve in LAC countries?	No, worsen	No	Yes
Do fiscal councils have effect?	Worsens	Worsens	Worsens
Do sovereign wealth funds have effect?	Improves	Improves	Improves
Short-term fiscal sustainability (debt)			
Is debt reduced?	No	No	No
Is debt reduced in smaller countries?	Yes	No	No
Is debt reduced in LAC countries?	No, increases debt	No	No
Do fiscal councils helps to reduce debt?	No, increases	Yes	Yes
Do sovereign wealth funds have effect?	Reduces	Reduces	Reducesr
Long-term fiscal sustainability (responsiveness of primary balance)			
Is the primary balance more responsive?	Yes	Yes	No
Is the primary balance more responsive in smaller countries?	No	More responsive	Responsive, but not significantly
Is the primary balance more responsive in LAC countries differently?	No	No	No

Sources: Schmidt-Hebbel and Soto 2017; Skrok et al. 2017.

Summary of Findings

Countries are increasingly using fiscal rules to strengthen fiscal discipline and stabilize short-term fluctuations in output, and smaller countries and the LAC region have followed this trend. By 2015 (latest available information), 92 countries had adopted fiscal rules; of these, 48 countries are large countries (representing 52 percent of these countries), while 44 are smaller (corresponding to 45 percent of smaller countries worldwide). In 2015 more than half of LAC countries (17 of the 33) had adopted fiscal rules. Small countries in LAC adopt fiscal rules in a similar proportion to other smaller countries in the rest of the world and in large LAC countries.

Globally, debt rules and balance rules are the most common, but expenditure rules and a combination of rules are increasingly used. Debt rules are the most common in smaller countries worldwide, LAC countries, and smaller LAC countries. In 2015 more than 70 debt rules and balance rules were in place in countries around the world. Although they are less common, the number of expenditure rules has risen sharply in recent years, from 23 in 2011 to 45 in 2015. Use of a combination of rules has become more common over time. More than 30 percent of smaller countries worldwide use a debt rule. Debt rules are also the most popular type of fiscal rule in both large and smaller countries in the LAC region.

However, the mere presence of fiscal rules does not guarantee compliance with them or, consequently, their effectiveness in achieving fiscal sustainability and smoothing output. The analysis done for this study reveals a significant gap between the adoption of fiscal rules and compliance with their provisions, which varies over time and among types of rules adopted, regions, and small and large countries. Compliance with all fiscal rules fell in the aftermath of the global financial crisis and recovered recently. Debt rules have had the highest compliance rates, and balance rules have had the lowest; however, compliance with expenditure rules has risen recently, and these rules now have the highest compliance rates.

There is no substantial difference in compliance rates between small and large countries, either LAC or non-LAC, but smaller LAC countries have significantly lower compliance. Average compliance rates in LAC countries are similar to those in other regions. There is also no significant difference in compliance between small and large countries globally. However, smaller LAC countries tend to comply less with fiscal rules than both large LAC countries and small countries in other regions.

A strong institutional and policy framework favors compliance with fiscal rules. The existence of enforcement mechanisms and the broad coverage of fiscal rules are both associated with higher compliance rates. Formal enforcement procedures such as automatic correction mechanisms, predetermined consequences for noncompliance, and clearly defined authority to take corrective action—appear to increase compliance. The scope of fiscal accounts regulated by the law is also associated with compliance.

Overall, fiscal rules improve fiscal balances, enhance debt sustainability, and reduce fiscal policy procyclicality, and these positive effects are reinforced when rules are actually complied with or when fiscal councils and sovereign wealth funds complement them. Globally, the presence of balance rules has a positive but statistically insignificant effect on fiscal balances, but this effect becomes significant among countries that comply with them. Countries with debt rules do not necessarily have lower debt levels. However, debt rules combined with fiscal councils are associated with a substantial reduction in public debt. Worldwide, countries that comply with their balance rules also exhibit a statistically significant reduction in debt levels. Both balance rules and debt rules are associated with improved debt sustainability, as they tend to increase the responsiveness of the primary balance to changes in the debt stock.

Expenditure rules are particularly effective in reducing expenditure procyclicality. Adopting and complying with expenditure rules tend to reduce expenditure procyclicality, and this effect is stronger when the expenditure rule is accompanied by a fiscal council or a sovereign wealth fund. Implementing an expenditure rule can reduce expenditure procyclicality by as much as 40 percent. The presence of enforcement mechanisms or other fiscal institutions enhances the stabilizing effect of expenditure rules.

Combining rules intensifies their positive impact on debt sustainability. Adopting a combination of fiscal rules—especially a combination of debt and expenditure rules or of debt and balance rules—is particularly effective in increasing the responsiveness of the primary balance to changes in the debt stock, thus ensuring debt sustainability.

Finally, with some exceptions, results also indicate that economic size does not have a significant impact on the effectiveness of fiscal rules, which implies that smaller countries that adopt and comply with fiscal rules can seize their benefits in the same way as larger countries.

Notes

This chapter is based on two background papers prepared for this study: Schmidt-Hebbel and Soto (2017) and Skrok et al. (2017).

1. For more detailed methodological aspects, see Schmidt-Hebbel and Soto (2017).

2. This type of rules can be applied to different categories of fiscal balances such as overall, primary or current balances.

3. Variations of structured balance rules are cyclically adjusted balance rules (CABRs), which correct the effect of business cycles on the fiscal balance, and over-the-cycle budget balance rules (OCBRs), which require the attainment of a nominal budget balance *on average* over the cycle and are multiyear rather than annual rules. The difference between structured balance rules and CABRs is that the former correct for one-time policy decisions and variations in commodity prices, while the latter correct only for output fluctuations affecting revenue and spending. In this regard, structured balance rules seem to be more suitable for countries that are highly exposed to commodity price shocks. The difference between OCBRs and structured balance rules and CABRs is the period of application of the limit they impose, which is not assessed annually but rather as an average over the years of a complete business cycle. This gives more flexibility for smoothing fluctuations, but OCBRs can be too loose or too tight at different phases of the business cycle, as their compliance will be assessed just after completion of the business cycle.

4. In 1998 the ECCU adopted a debt ceiling and budget rules to support its currency union. ECCU members are Antigua and Barbuda, Dominica, Grenada, St. Kitts and Nevis, St. Lucia, and St. Vincent and the Grenadines.

5. Given the small number of structural balance rules worldwide and in LAC and the fact that they have been adopted only recently, throughout this chapter, budget balance rules and structural balance rules are not differentiated; both are covered in the balance rules group. In the same vein, due to the small number, revenue rules are not included in the analysis presented here.

6. This section is based on Skrok et al. (2017).

7. The analysis is restricted to legally codified national fiscal rules that apply to the central or general government budget and that have been in place for at least three consecutive years. Subnational and supranational fiscal rules are excluded. Revenue rules are excluded because they are relatively uncommon, while the smaller number of structural balance rules are included in the broader category of balance rules.

8. Several attempts have been made to calculate FRSIs. One of the most popular approaches was created by the Directorate General for Economic and Financial Affairs of the European Commission. For this study, the World Bank's team calculated the FRSI for each fiscal rule based on information presented by the IMF (2015) describing several dimensions (monitoring of compliance outside government, formal enforcement procedures, coverage, legal basis, and escape clause). All variables from the IMF (2015) database were normalized before the indexes were calculated.

9. The analysis prepared for this study by Schmidt-Hebbel and Soto (2018) confirms the influence of these structural factors.

10. The results given in this section are drawn from Schmidt-Hebbel and Soto (2018).

11. In the case of fiscal balances, fiscal rules that reduce procyclical fiscal policies favor a positive relation between budget balances and GDP fluctuations: a higher fiscal balance whenever the economy expands reflects an output-stabilizing fiscal stance.

12. In this study, debt sustainability is measured by the responsiveness of the primary balance to changes in the debt-to-GDP ratio. This way to measure fiscal sustainability was initially proposed by Bohn (1998).

References

Auerbach, Alan J. 2014. *Fiscal Uncertainty and How to Deal with It.* Working Paper 6, Hutchins Center on Monetary and Fiscal Policy, Brookings Institution, Washington, DC.

Bohn, Henning. 1998. "The Behavior of U.S Public Debt and Deficits." *Quarterly Journal of Economics* 113 (3): 949–63.

Bova, Elva, Tidiane Kinda, Priscilla Muthoora, and Frederik Toscan. 2015. "Fiscal Rules at a Glance." IMF Staff Paper, International Monetary Fund, Washington, DC.

Commonwealth Secretariat and World Bank. 2000. "Commonwealth Secretariat/World Bank Joint Task Force in Small States." Small States: Economic Review and Basic Statistics, vol. 5, Commonwealth Secretariat, London. https://doi.org/10.14217/smalst-2000-en.

Cordes, Till, Tidiane Kinda, Priscilla S. Muthoora, and Anke Weber. 2015. "Expenditure Rules: Effective Tools for Sound Fiscal Policy." IMF Working Paper 15/29, International Monetary Fund, Washington, DC.

Debrun, Xavier, Laurent Moulin, Alessandro Turrini, Joaquim Ayuso-i-Casals, and Manmohan S. Kumar. 2008. "Tied to the Mast? National Fiscal Rules in the European Union." *Economic Policy* 23 (54): 299–362.

Debrun, Xavier, Tidiane Kinda, Teresa Curristine, Luc Eyraud, Jason Harris, and Johann Seiwald. 2013. "The Functions and Impact of Fiscal Councils." IMF Policy Paper, International Monetary Fund, Washington, DC.

European Commission. 2009. "Fiscal Rules, Independent Institutions, and Medium-Term Budgetary Frameworks." In *Public Finance in EMU—2009*, part II.2.4, 87–99. Brussels: European Commission.

Fall, Falilou, Debra Bloch, Jean-Marc Fournier, and Peter Hoeller. 2015. "Prudent Debt Targets and Fiscal Frameworks." OECD Economic Policy Paper 15, OECD Publishing, Paris.

Heinemann, Frederich, Marc-Daniel Moessinger, and Mustafa Yeter. 2016. "Do Fiscal Rules Constrain Fiscal Policy? A Meta-Regression-Analysis." ZEW Discussion Paper 16-027, Leibniz Centre for European Economic Research (ZEW), Mannheim.

Iara, Anna, and Guntram Wolff. 2011. "Rules and Risk in the Euro Area." Bruegel Working Paper 2011/10, Bruegel, Brussels.

IMF (International Monetary Fund). 2015. Fiscal Rules Dataset. Washington, DC: IMF.

Kopits, George, and Steven Symansky. 1998. "Fiscal Rules." IMF Occasional Paper 162, International Monetary Fund, Washington, DC.

Marneffe, Wim, Bas Van Aarle, Wouter Van der Wielen, and Lode Vereecl. 2011. "The Impact of Fiscal Rules on Public Finances: Theory and Empirical Evidence for the Euro Area." CESifo DICE Report, vol. 3, CESifo Economic Studies, Oxford University, Oxford.

Nerlich, Carolin, and Wolf H. Reuter. 2013. "The Design of National Fiscal Frameworks and Their Budgetary Impact." Working Paper 1588, European Central Bank, Frankfurt.

Schmidt-Hebbel, Klaus, and Raimundo Soto. 2017. "Fiscal Rules and Fiscal Performance: World Evidence." Documentos de Trabajo 517, Instituto de Economia, Pontificia Universidad Católica de Chile. https://ideas.repec.org/p/ioe/doctra/517.html.

Schmidt-Hebbel, Klaus, and Raimundo Soto. 2018. "Fiscal Performance, Fiscal Rules, and Country Size." Background paper, World Bank, Washington, DC.

Skrok, Emilia, Jan Gąska, Paulina Hołda, and Friederike Koehler-Geib. 2017. "Having or Complying with Fiscal Rules? Insights for Small Countries in LAC." Background paper, World Bank, Washington, DC.

Wyplosz, Charles. 2013. "Fiscal Rules: Theoretical Issues and Historical Experiences." In *Fiscal Policy after the Crisis,* edited by Alberto Alesina and Francesco Giavazzi, 496–525. Chicago: University of Chicago Press.

3
Designing Effective Fiscal Rules in Smaller Countries

Fiscal rules are typically aimed at ensuring debt sustainability. However, in recent decades they have also been designed with the aim of smoothing output fluctuations. Fiscal rules can help to manage the growth of public spending and, in conjunction with sovereign wealth funds, can promote intergenerational equity. Debt rules and budget balance rules focus on achieving debt sustainability but tend to exacerbate the procyclicality of spending and fluctuations in output. Structural balance rules focus on stabilizing output but contribute less to debt sustainability. They seem to be the most effective type of rule for attenuating cyclical volatility and smoothing household consumption over time. From that perspective, they seem to be more effective for enhancing intertemporal welfare and to be well suited to the needs of smaller economies facing higher volatility.

There are, however, some caveats. For example, persistent shocks, higher initial debt levels, and imperfect credit markets reduce the effectiveness of structural balance rules in smoothing shocks. Moreover, structural balance rules are technically and institutionally harder to implement, monitor, and maintain and are difficult to communicate. Capacity constraints and transparency issues can hamper their implementation and credibility. From this perspective, the adoption of a combination of expenditure rules with debt rules or expenditure rules with budget balance rules (with well-defined escape clauses) can have the same effects, with more simplicity and transparency.

Introduction

Fiscal rules can greatly enhance macroeconomic management in smaller countries, but their effectiveness hinges on the ability of policy makers to identify the patterns of business cycles. The particularities of the business cycles and shocks faced by smaller countries can affect the effectiveness of fiscal rules. While some fiscal rules support debt sustainability, they can also exacerbate the amplitude of economic cycles.

95

Furthermore, fiscal rules aimed at stabilizing economic fluctuations in countries with highly persistent shocks or asymmetric business cycles may result in unsustainable debt or the accumulation of excessive savings, with negative welfare effects.

In particular, as shown in chapter 1, smaller countries tend to have more volatile and asymmetric business cycles marked by deeper contractions and shorter expansions. They tend to face more persistent shocks, have larger public sectors relative to their economic size, adopt more procyclical fiscal policies, and experience greater volatility in their gross domestic product (GDP), gross national income (GNI), fiscal balances, and unemployment levels. Furthermore, smaller economies are more exposed to terms-of-trade shocks, which tend to be more persistent than GDP shocks. Fiscal policy is often the only stabilizing instrument available to smaller countries, which tend to have limited monetary policy flexibility and are more likely to use common regional currencies or exchange rate pegs. Fiscal rules can be especially useful in creating a more predictable fiscal policy framework and building buffers against adverse economic shocks.

Well-designed fiscal rules and supportive fiscal frameworks are essential elements of a transparent, predictable, and sustainable fiscal policy that anchors the economy and attenuates economic fluctuations. Fiscal responsibility laws, fiscal rules and escape clauses, medium-term fiscal frameworks, and fiscal councils form the main elements of a fiscal framework. Fiscal rules can make fiscal policy more predictable, enhancing the government's overall policy credibility, which in turn can facilitate access to financial markets and increase the government's ability to leverage those markets to support macroeconomic stabilization. While not strictly necessary, sovereign wealth funds are an auxiliary fiscal policy instrument that can strengthen the functioning of transparent, predictable, and sustainable fiscal rules and support intergenerational fairness.

This chapter offers analytical criteria for assessing what types of fiscal rules are best suited to the needs and macroeconomic conditions of smaller countries. It provides analytical underpinnings for the choice of fiscal rules based on quantitative assessments of their benefits and costs in terms of fiscal sustainability and intertemporal welfare. The effects of fiscal rules on debt sustainability, output smoothing, and households' intertemporal welfare depend on the characteristics of the business cycle, which, in turn, vary with the size of the economy. The persistence of shocks, the amplitude and duration of upturns and downturns of the business cycle, and the sources of volatility to be addressed are critical for the choice of fiscal rules and their technical design. In addition, initial levels of indebtedness and technical and institutional capacities in each country also provide relevant criteria for a sensible selection of fiscal rules.

The chapter is organized in three sections. The first section discusses the main objectives of fiscal rules and briefly describes how ancillary policy tools such as escape clauses and sovereign funds can enhance their intended effects. The second section examines how different fiscal rules interact with the specific characteristics of the business cycle in smaller economies to affect fiscal policy and household welfare. Finally, the third section summarizes the analytical criteria for designing fiscal rules in smaller economies.

Objectives of Fiscal Rules

The prime objective of fiscal rules is to ensure debt sustainability. Rules-based approaches have been established to mitigate the inherent deficit bias of fiscal policy, which reflects a time-inconsistency problem.[1] In the absence of time inconsistency, negative fiscal balances during downturns may be followed by surpluses during upturns, ensuring debt sustainability in the long run. However, during upturns, fiscal authorities may have few incentives to generate surpluses and savings. By applying numerical norms to debt levels, fiscal balances, or other key fiscal aggregates, fiscal rules lessen the deficit bias and reinforce the commitment of policy makers to debt sustainability.

More recently, fiscal rules have also been envisaged as a mechanism for smoothing fluctuations in output, serving as a social insurance instrument, and promoting intergenerational fairness. Fiscal rules can also help to stabilize economic fluctuations by enabling acyclical or countercyclical fiscal responses and mitigating fluctuations in output and consumption associated with business and commodity price cycles. Smoothing fluctuations in output is especially important for vulnerable groups that are less able to cope with negative income shocks because they do not have the ability to save, do not have access to credit, and are more likely to rely on government spending and transfers. Moreover, fiscal rules in conjunction with sovereign wealth funds, which enable the accumulation of nonrenewable resources, also can favor intergenerational equity.

Fiscal rules also can help to slow down the growth of public spending. By setting numerical constraints on the growth of public spending, fiscal rules can also be useful for controlling the size of government. Rules that set ceilings for revenues also prevent the growth of government size and excessive tax burdens. Setting caps on spending growth linked to potential output shields public spending from output or revenue volatility and has positive effects on output stabilization. As a result, rules that isolate spending from fluctuations help to protect vulnerable groups from income fluctuations.

Fiscal rules can also be considered a social insurance instrument due to their ability to smooth income fluctuations for the most vulnerable groups. Fiscal rules that help to reduce deviations from consumption smoothing arising from fluctuations in output, by either stabilizing the economic cycle or avoiding reductions in spending during recessions, provide social insurance. This insurance has a stronger impact on groups that are most affected by income fluctuations, do not have access to credit markets to smooth temporary fluctuations on their incomes, or benefit more from public goods and services or receive government transfers (Aguirre 2017, 2018; Engel, Nielson, and Valdés 2013).

While fiscal rules can enable countries to pursue fiscal sustainability and output stabilization simultaneously, the achievement of these two objectives may face important trade-offs. A rules-based commitment to long-term debt sustainability can provide governments with the fiscal space necessary to address cyclical downturns and macroeconomic shocks without resorting to unsustainable deficit spending. However, pursuing debt sustainability by imposing targets for the debt or fiscal balance may compromise the ability of fiscal policy to support output stabilization in the short run. Conversely, efforts to insulate government spending from fluctuations in revenue or the adoption of countercyclical fiscal responses to attenuate the effects of persistent shocks may harm fiscal sustainability.

Debt rules and budget balance rules are tightly linked to debt sustainability, but they may negatively affect output stabilization, as they can foster a procyclical fiscal stance. Figure 3.1 illustrates the impact of the different types of fiscal rules on fiscal sustainability, output stabilization, social insurance, and controlling the size of government. Regarding output shocks, budget balance rules and debt rules typically provide the lowest degree of cyclical flexibility. Moreover, they tend to exacerbate economic expansions and contractions, as they enforce debt or budget balance targets without regard to the business cycle. Given their procyclical nature, debt rules and budget balance rules have ambiguous effects on the size of government. They may have

FIGURE 3.1: **Types of Fiscal Rules and Objectives**

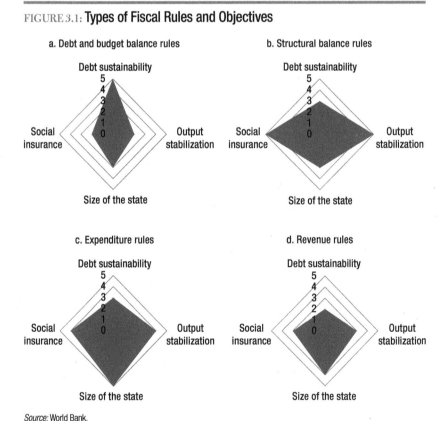

Source: World Bank.

negative impacts on the social insurance role of fiscal policy, as they often impose spending cuts to address revenue shortfalls during downturns.

Expenditure rules aim to control the size of government and have positive effects on output smoothing, as they turn spending acyclical. However, their effects on fiscal sustainability are ambiguous and depend on whether the economy is in an expansion or a recession. By capping the growth of public spending, expenditure rules effectively control the size of government. They insulate the evolution of government spending from cyclical fluctuations and have positive effects on output stabilization. Indeed, they do not require spending adjustments to cyclical or discretionary reductions in tax revenues and thus do not restrict the economic stabilization function of fiscal policy in times of adverse shocks. Even greater countercyclicality can be achieved by excluding automatic stabilizers such as spending categories (unemployment insurance) from the caps on spending growth. However, this may come at the expense of debt sustainability objectives. Through their effect on the stability of spending and output fluctuations, expenditure rules can enable fiscal policy to exert a social insurance role, helping to smooth consumption of population groups that are unable to attenuate fluctuations in their incomes and resulting in positive effects on equity. By making government spending acyclical, they have positive effects on debt sustainability during upturns but deteriorating impacts on fiscal balances during downturns. Therefore, expenditure rules have no clear effects on fiscal sustainability unless combined with a debt or a budget balance rule.

Revenue rules set floors or caps on government revenue collection that contain the size of government, but they have an ambiguous impact on debt sustainability and can have a negative effect on output stabilization. Revenue rules that set floors for government revenues aim to ensure that adequate revenue is available to finance government operations and critical service delivery. Revenue rules that impose ceilings on government revenues prevent the tax burden from becoming excessive. However, they do not limit spending, revenue floors are not binding in upturns, and revenue caps are not binding in downturns; therefore, revenue rules do not affect fiscal balances and debt in a clear direction. However, they do not generally account for the effect of automatic stabilizers on the revenue side in a downturn or the impact of revenue ceilings in an upturn. Because automatic stabilizers are stronger on the revenue side, these rules tend to result in a procyclical fiscal policy that undermines the stabilizing and social insurance effects of fiscal policy.

Countries often use a combination of fiscal rules to achieve multiple objectives or reinforce their effects. As shown in chapter 2, the most common combinations of rules are a budget balance rule coupled with a debt rule and a debt rule coupled with an expenditure rule. Combining a debt rule with a budget balance rule reinforces their effects on debt sustainability and provides operational guidance when actual debt levels are far from the targeted levels set by the debt rule. Debt ceilings only constrain fiscal balances when debt levels are close to the established ceiling; when debt levels are far from the ceiling, imposing a numerical target on the annual budget balance consistent with the long-term ceiling defined by the debt rule can serve as a short-term binding constraint on fiscal balances.

Combining a debt rule with an expenditure rule or a debt rule with a budget balance rule that includes a well-defined escape clause can mimic the properties of a structural balance rule. During economic expansions, when positive budget balances are easier to achieve, the expenditure ceiling is the binding constraint, preventing procyclical expenditures from exacerbating the amplitude of the business cycle. During downturns, the budget balance rule or the debt rule becomes the binding constraint. This can increase procyclicality, as expenditures need to be reduced to achieve the budget balance rule or debt rule target. However, an escape clause can allow the authorities to increase or decrease the numerical target value of the budget balance rule, increase that of the debt rule, or enable the expenditure rule to continue functioning to avoid procyclical expenditure cuts.

The adoption of a structural balance rule together with a debt rule may simultaneously support output stabilization and debt sustainability but will weaken the stabilization effects of the structural balance rule. One of the concerns with the adoption of structural balance rules is that they may lead to an unsustainable debt path in scenarios of persistent negative shocks or very asymmetric cycles. The adoption of a debt rule together with a structural balance rule is expected to address debt sustainability concerns and enhance the credibility of the fiscal policy. If debt levels are well below the debt ceiling set in the debt rule, the structural balance rule will operate fully and stabilize outputs. However, debt levels close to the debt ceiling may compromise the functioning of the structural balance rule and weaken its output stabilization effects, as the debt ceiling becomes the binding constraint and debt sustainability criteria determine expenditure adjustments.

While the combination of fiscal rules may promote positive complementary effects or reinforce intended effects, applying too many fiscal rules simultaneously can excessively constrain fiscal policy and create conflicting effects. As fiscal rules constrain policy, the excess of rules may substantially reduce the space for fiscal policy maneuvers and engender rigidity. Moreover, the proliferation of rules makes the simultaneous fulfillment of them increasingly difficult. The combination of several rules may also generate conflicting effects. For instance, rules that set revenue floors or ceilings or earmark revenue for specific expenditures can increase procyclicality.

While well-designed fiscal rules can provide adequate flexibility to deal with most shocks, escape clauses may ensure that there is enough flexibility to deal with larger shocks or one-time events. Escape clauses allow temporary deviations from the rule during infrequent and strong shocks (for example, natural disasters, financial system crisis, or deep recessions) or to address the budgetary impacts of major shocks (for example, a bailout of the banking system). They also can allow for the implementation of public sector reforms (for example, civil service or pension reforms) that might be costly in the short term but are expected to have long-term positive fiscal effects. To ensure that the integrity of the rule is not undermined, having predetermined, credible, and transparent mechanisms underpinning the escape clause is critical. Specifically, there should be (a) a very limited range of factors that trigger the escape clause; (b) clear guidelines for the interpretation of events; and (c) a provision that specifies the path back to the fiscal rule (Schaechter et al. 2012). Formal escape clause provisions are found mostly in more recently introduced rules. Escape clauses are more common in budget balance rules, debt rules, and expenditure rules, allowing for temporary deviations from the rules in case of a recession or a significant slowdown in growth. While structural balance rules provide flexibility to attenuate output shocks, natural disasters, and financial crises, deep recessions and public sector reforms are one-time events (at least not recurrent events) that are better addressed by escape clauses. Therefore, structural balance rules also may be accompanied by well-defined escape clauses to enhance its output stabilizing effects (box 3.1).

Sovereign wealth funds make the functioning of fiscal rules more transparent, but they need to be framed within the broader structure of the management of fiscal policy, including the fiscal rule and the overall fiscal policy framework. The proper

---

BOX 3.1: **Establishing Well-Defined Escape Clauses**

To be resilient and credible, a rules-based fiscal framework must be sufficiently flexible, while remaining simple and transparent. A useful distinction can be made between predictable events that invariably occur after some time—such as business cycle fluctuations—and unpredictable realizations of macroeconomic or other events with massive fiscal implications. The latter must be addressed with well-defined escape clauses, whereas the former can be handled with an adequate definition of the fiscal indicators subject to a numerical limit. Because output stabilization is both harder to achieve in low-income countries and small economies (given the difficulties in correctly identifying business cycles) and less of a concern than other objectives of fiscal policy, the rule's *flexibility* would come primarily in the form of well-designed escape clauses, including clauses for natural disasters or other large shocks.

However, to preserve credibility, the escape clause should be very well defined, and the transition path toward resumption of the rule should be clearly articulated. This is a critical aspect, as many countries have adopted fiscal rules with ill-defined escape clauses that leave too much scope for governmental discretion in triggering them and are vague about the resumption path. To ensure that the credibility of the rule is not undermined, the escape clause should define (a) the type or types of shocks that allow for the escape clause to be triggered, which should be very limited; (b) the exact magnitude of the shock(s), with numerical measures; (c) clear guidelines for the interpretation of events; and (d) the path back to the fiscal rule, with clearly articulated timing and numerical targets.

(continued on next page)

BOX 3.1: Establishing Well-Defined Escape Clauses *(continued)*

Escape clauses are also applied to the rules for operating sovereign wealth funds. In this case, escape clauses suspend the fund's accumulation or disbursement rules to deal with extraordinary situations, such as a nationwide natural disaster, a state of emergency, or some other other large, unexpected shock. These clauses need to be defined strictly to ensure their proper use and could be complemented by a medium-term plan to replenish the fund.

In Latin America and the Caribbean, fiscal rules in Colombia, Grenada, Jamaica, Panama, and Peru have well-defined escape clauses that specify a narrow set of events that trigger their use, precisely define the magnitude of the shocks and the deviation allowed, and establish the period and path of the adjustment in the aftermath of the shock. For example, in Panama escape clauses were triggered in 2009 (when the global financial crisis brought a slowdown of GDP growth of 1 percent) and in 2011 (natural disaster). Accordingly, the deficit ceilings of 2009 and 2011 were raised from 1 percent to 2.5 percent and then to 3 percent of GDP. The rule establishes a period of three years of linear adjustment (one-third per year) for a slowdown in economic growth, provided the rate of growth of GDP is less than 2 percent; it only applies for one year for a natural disaster.

integration of a sovereign wealth fund with the overall fiscal framework can be achieved by linking the flows to and from the fund to the overall fiscal balance. Indeed, the fund's balance should be a "mirror image" of the government's budget or structural balance. In the context of the budget, a sovereign wealth fund needs to respect the integrity of the budget process, meaning that it should not have authority to spend and its outflows should go through the national budget. Policies and rules for a sovereign wealth fund's funding, withdrawal, and spending operations should be clear and consistent with the purposes of the fiscal rule that it supports (box 3.2).[2]

Comparing the Welfare Effects of Fiscal Rules in Smaller Economies

From an analytical perspective, determining the most appropriate fiscal rules requires a thorough comparison of their welfare effects over time. Many analytical models assess fiscal rules in terms of their ability to promote output stabilization when the real effects of government spending on output are substantial (González, Muñoz, and Schmidt-Hebbel 2013; Kumhof and Laxton 2013; Medina and Soto 2016; Pieschacón 2012). Welfare is typically linked to the stability of intertemporal consumption, and the welfare effects of different fiscal rules reflect the extent to which they tend to smooth consumption over time.

Key Principles for Establishing a Savings Fund to Address High Volatility in Smaller Economies

Key fiscal principles

- A strong link is needed between the fund's accumulation and use mechanisms and the fiscal rule that helps to smooth the high volatility.

- Accumulation and withdrawals should be clearly stated and based on specific but simple rules, consistent with the design of the fiscal rule and the medium-term fiscal framework.

- While accumulation rules should be linked to a general fiscal rule, withdrawal rules could be also be crafted in alignment with the "escape clause" and be set in motion by triggers such as the severity of the shock or natural disaster. Clear quantitative criteria for triggering withdrawals should be identified.

- In many cases, an initial capitalization will be needed so that buffers are sufficient to address early shocks.

- After the initial capitalization, the country will need to generate fiscal savings through the fiscal rule to gain credibility and gather further support externally when needed and feasible. This not only will create a virtuous cycle and incentive framework but also could improve a country's credit rating, reduce borrowing costs, and improve debt dynamics.

Key governance principles

- Broad political commitment to sustainability of the design of the framework needs to be established, including fiscal discipline to adhere to the adopted framework.

- The management of the fund needs to be integrated effectively into the fiscal policy framework.

- A clear structure of checks and balances and oversight mechanisms is needed to ensure sound management of the fund.

- The legislation should outline a clear division of responsibilities between the owner and operational manager and emphasize that the operational management shall be carried out in a professional manner, independent of any political interference.

- The ministry of finance could be the owner of the fund on behalf of government and delegate authority (independence) to the operational manager by adopting policies and issuing regulations, rules, and procedures for the delegation of power and responsibilities, the investment policy, risk management requirements, reporting requirements, and internal and external audits.

(continued on next page)

BOX 3.2: Key Principles for Establishing a Savings Fund to Address High Volatility in Smaller Economies *(continued)*

- If a fiscal council is to advise on withdrawals from the fund, it should be independent and separate from the sovereign wealth fund's board, committee, or council for the management of assets to avoid conflicts of interest.

- Clear rules and procedures are needed for internal control and audits as well as independent external audits, complying with the Santiago principles.

In Latin America and the Caribbean, 17 sovereign wealth funds have been established, including in Bolivia, Brazil (terminated), Chile (two funds), Colombia, Ecuador (terminated), Grenada, Guyana, Mexico (three funds), Panama, Peru, St. Vincent and the Grenadines, Suriname, and the República Bolivariana de Venezuela (two funds). Sovereign wealth funds in Chile, Colombia, Guyana, Panama, and Peru were established by legislation; have well-defined, clear rules of accumulation and disbursement; and are well integrated with the budget and fiscal rules.

The optimality of a fiscal rule is measured by its ability to reduce expenditure procyclicality, attenuate fiscal volatility, and smooth consumption. Aguirre (2017) developed an analytical model for this study that compares the welfare effects of structural balance rules and budget balance rules using parameters that take into consideration the characteristics of small economies.[3] From a welfare perspective, the rationale for adopting fiscal rules is to stabilize household consumption by ensuring the provision of public goods and services and the transfer of payments to households. While the welfare gains generated by smoothing fluctuations in the business cycle are significant, they vary substantially across households at different income levels, particularly those that are more vulnerable to unemployment during downturns and that cannot borrow or insure themselves. For those households, reducing the procyclicality of spending and transfers and easing fiscal volatility have highly positive welfare effects. Analyzing the impact of shocks at both the individual and aggregate levels reveals large welfare gains from eliminating the source of aggregate fluctuations; however, the benefits vary across individuals according to their education level, employment status, annual income, and net wealth.

In this regard, structural balance rules can reap significant welfare gains, especially for asset-poor individuals who are vulnerable to unemployment shocks and lack access to credit markets. By promoting acyclical fiscal policies, structural balance rules enhance welfare by stabilizing output and consumption and reinforce the social insurance role of fiscal policy. In a context of strong volatility of output and high procyclicality and volatility of government spending, structural balance rules are the most appropriate type of fiscal rule, as they are better at isolating spending from fluctuations in revenue and output. Because they eliminate the procyclicality of government spending and reduce its volatility, they are particularly beneficial for low-income households. Welfare gains from adopting structural balance rules can be as large as 0.6 percent of consumption equivalent for poor households that are exposed to long periods of unemployment and are unable to insure themselves due to their lack of access to credit (figure 3.2, panel a).

The welfare gains generated by budget balance rules are also positive and higher for individuals who are exposed to unemployment and unable to borrow to smooth income fluctuations, but these gains are smaller than those generated by structural balance rules. Although government spending is still highly procyclical under budget balance rules, it is less procyclical than the spending observed in smaller countries. Therefore, the welfare gains of adopting budget balance rules come from the reduction of spending procyclicality, and the transition is particularly welfare enhancing for individuals who have few assets or are especially vulnerable to employment shocks. However, as budget balance rules require spending to be consistent with revenues in any period,[4] government spending under budget balance rules is more volatile than what is normally observed in smaller countries. Higher volatility of spending translates into higher volatility of consumption for mostly asset-poor individuals who have a high propensity to consume and are credit constrained. This higher volatility of consumption rapidly reduces the benefits gained from lower procyclicality of the stock of assets (figure 3.2, panel b).

Welfare gains from adopting budget balance rules can be larger if revenue volatility is reduced by the establishment of a sovereign wealth fund. Reducing revenue volatility through a structural balance rule does not generate additional welfare

---

FIGURE 3.2: **Welfare Gains from Adopting Structural Balance Rules or Budget Balance Rules**

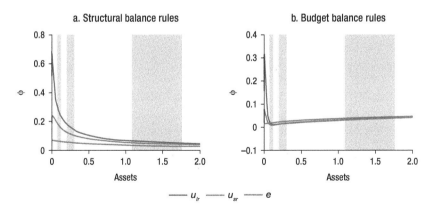

a. Structural balance rules

b. Budget balance rules

$$\_\_\_ u_{lr} \quad \_\_\_ u_{sr} \quad \_\_\_ e$$

Source: Aguirre 2017.
Note: Φ = consumption gains, in percentage points, of moving to structural balance rules (left) or budget balance rules (right). The horizontal axis shows the amount of assets as a fraction of annual income per capita. Shaded bars show the range of assets held by agents belonging to the second tercile of each efficiency group's wealth distribution. Gains are evaluated at the average level of capital and debt under R, and the rest of the state variables are weighted according to their stationary distributions.

FIGURE 3.3: **Welfare Gains from Reducing Revenue Volatility with Structural Balance Rules or Budget Balance Rules**

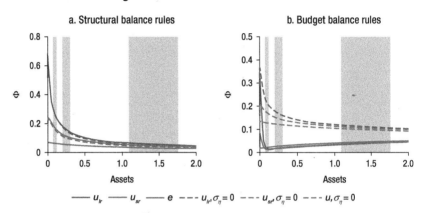

Source: Aguirre 2017.
Note: Φ = consumption gains, in percentage points, of moving to structural balance rules (left) or budget balance rules (right). The horizontal axis shows the amount of assets as a fraction of annual income per capita. Shaded bars show the range of assets held by agents belonging to the second tercile of each efficiency group's wealth distribution. Gains are evaluated at the average level of capital and debt under R, and the rest of the state variables are weighted according to their stationary distributions.

gains, since the rule already isolates spending from temporary fluctuations in revenue (figure 3.3, panel a). Additional welfare effects of reducing revenue volatility are larger with a budget balance rule. Indeed, an important policy implication regarding the higher volatility of spending embedded in a budget balance rule is that the operation of a sovereign wealth fund can reduce revenue volatility and enlarge rather than offset the positive effects of the lower procyclicality of spending associated with a budget balance rule (figure 3.3, panel b). In this case, the numerical target of the budget balance rule should be consistent with the accumulation of assets in the sovereign wealth fund and should apply an escape clause enabling use of the assets when there are revenue shortfalls. This is particularly important, as small countries (especially very small economies) face much higher volatility of revenue.[5]

Indeed, the welfare impact of fiscal rules is related directly to their ability to reduce spending procyclicality; for this reason, expenditure rules may replicate gains similar to those of structural balance rules. Fiscal rules produce greater welfare gains when a country's initial fiscal stance is highly procyclical (figure 3.4). Shifting from very procyclical to acyclical fiscal policies or at least less procyclical policies generates the greatest benefits for vulnerable households that experience longer periods of unemployment and tend to rely most heavily on transfers from government. Because expenditure rules make spending acyclical, their benefits are commensurate with the benefits generated by structural balance rules.

Welfare Gains from Adopting Structural Balance Rules or Budget Balance Rules with an Initial Procyclicality of 1.15

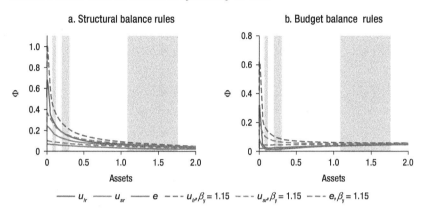

a. Structural balance rules b. Budget balance rules

Source: Aguirre 2017.
Note: β_y = 1.15 is the value of the coefficient of spending to GDP for the 75th percentile of the distribution of fiscal procyclicality in small countries. Φ = consumption gains, in percentage points, of moving to structural balance rules (left) or budget balance rules (right). The horizontal axis shows the amount of assets as a fraction of annual income per capita. Shaded bars show the range of assets held by agents belonging to the second tercile of each efficiency group's wealth distribution. Gains are evaluated at the average level of capital and debt under R, and the rest of the state variables are weighted according to their stationary distributions.

While structural balance rules seem to generate larger welfare gains than budget balance rules, characteristics of the business cycle in smaller economies can alter this finding. Indeed, the features of business cycles in smaller economies highlighted in chapter 2 have critical implications for the ability of structural balance rules and budget balance rules to smooth fluctuations in output and consumption and enhance welfare. High output volatility, asymmetric business cycles, high and volatile unemployment rates, elevated revenue volatility, greater expenditure procyclicality, and relatively large public sectors are features of small economies that influence the effectiveness of structural balance rules and budget balance rules in ensuring debt sustainability and output stabilization.

Structural balance rules and budget balance rules yield larger benefits in economies subject to asymmetric business cycles, but structural balance rules can lead to unsustainable indebtedness if shocks are asymmetric. During asymmetric cycles, which are characterized by deeper recessions and shorter upturns and are common in smaller economies,[6] the ability of structural balance rules (and budget balance rules) to eliminate (mitigate) the need for expenditure cuts during recessions is especially valuable. The welfare gains for individuals experiencing protracted unemployment are more than double the gains estimated in the baseline scenario (figure 3.5). During deep recessions, when unemployment rates are high, the welfare effects of stabilizing policies tend to be especially significant for low-skill workers who are subject to longer

FIGURE 3.5: **Welfare Gains from Adopting Structural Balance Rules or Budget Balance Rules in a Context of Asymmetric Shocks**

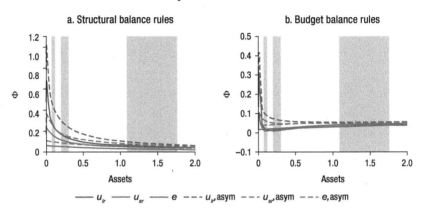

a. Structural balance rules   b. Budget balance rules

$$u_{lr} \quad u_{sr} \quad e \quad u_{lr}\,\text{asym} \quad u_{sr}\,\text{asym} \quad e,\text{asym}$$

Source: Aguirre 2017.

Note: Φ = consumption gains, in percentage points, of moving to a structural balance rule (left) and a budget balance rule (right). The horizontal axis shows the amount of assets as a fraction of annual income per capita. Shaded bars show the range of assets held by agents belonging to the second tercile of each efficiency group's wealth distribution. Gains are evaluated at the average level of capital and debt under R, and the rest of the state variables are weighted according to their stationary distributions.

periods of unemployment, reinforcing the social insurance role of fiscal policy. However, acyclical spending stances during long recessions and short expansions can undermine fiscal sustainability. Structural balance rules in countries with these business cycle characteristics can lead to excessive borrowing.

More important, structural balance rules are far less advantageous for small countries facing persistent commodity price shocks, and using structural balance rules to attenuate persistent shocks may be unsustainable. Pennings and Mendes (2017) developed a model for this study to assess the welfare effects of several fiscal rules, including structural balance rules and budget balance rules, under commodity price shocks of varying levels of persistence.[7] Attempting to use a structural balance rule to smooth persistent shocks can be counterproductive and unsustainable. If negative commodity price shocks persist, a structural balance rule will postpone adjustments in consumption for financially constrained agents and delay fiscal consolidation, which may cause debt dynamics to become unsustainable, as the government sells assets or accumulates debt to finance a budgetary shortfall that, for practical purposes, may be permanent. Conversely, if positive commodity price shocks persist, a structural balance rule may cause public assets to increase indefinitely, deferring increases in consumption ineffectively. Welfare losses are lower under budget balance rules than structural balance rules if shocks have a persistence value greater than 0.9 (figure 3.6).

Budget balance rules can outperform structural balance rules when commodity price shocks are highly persistent. In these scenarios, governments are not required to smooth economic shocks. Although many commodity price shocks are very persistent

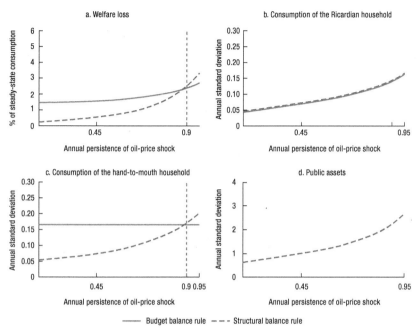

a. Welfare loss

b. Consumption of the Ricardian household

c. Consumption of the hand-to-mouth household

d. Public assets

——— Budget balance rule   – – – Structural balance rule

Source: Pennings and Mendes 2017.

(that is, they have persistence values approaching 1), persistence tends to vary by commodity. For instance, oil and gas shocks tend to be persistent, implying that oil and gas exporters should adopt more procyclical fiscal rules, such as budget balance rules. By contrast, agricultural exporters, which face less persistent shocks, should adopt rules that favor acyclical spending, such as structural balance rules. Governments that capture a greater share of commodity revenues that have more persistent shocks tend to benefit from fiscal rules that allow for more procyclicality (table 3.1).

Budget balance rules can also be superior to structural balance rules when persistent commodity price shocks have large spillover effects on the nonresource economy. Commodity prices and nonresource GDP tend to be closely correlated in smaller countries due to their limited economic diversification. If government assets increase with commodity prices, interest rates fall and investment rises (in a model with reduced-form financial frictions) (figure 3.7). Consequently, nonresource GDP tends to increase when commodity prices are high and to decrease when commodity price shocks are negative. In this scenario of highly persistent commodity price shocks with strong spillovers to the rest of the economy, the optimal fiscal response to commodity price shocks is more procyclical as budget

TABLE 3.1: Persistence of Commodity Price Shocks and Optimal Expenditure Response, by Commodity

Commodity	Persistence (ρ) [Half-life], annual	Optimal spending out of extra US$1 in revenues ($\theta_\mu$)*
Petroleum	0.94 [11.1 years]	0.73
Oil and natural Gas combined	0.93 [9.5 years]	0.68
Beef	0.90 [6.6 years]	0.56
Natural gas, copper, gold, coffee (Robusta)	0.89 [6 years]	0.53
Soybeans	0.87 [5 years]	0.48
Bananas	0.8 [3 years]	0.35
Coffee (Arabica)	0.77 [2.6 years]	0.31
Sugar	0.74 [2.3 years]	0.28

Source: Pennings and Mendes 2017.

balance rules generate greater welfare gains than structural balance rules. However, this does not imply that procyclical fiscal responses are the optimal response to temporary shocks. Even if shocks to nonresource GDP are highly persistent, the government can still respond acyclically or countercyclically to nonresource GDP shocks and respond procyclically to the underlying commodity price shock.

High initial debt levels also reduce the effectiveness of structural balance rules. The welfare gains from moving to a structural balance rule decrease with debt levels, as higher debt reduces the fiscal space for smoothing downturns. A negative output shock increases debt-to-GDP ratios, and a lower increase or even a decrease in spending may be needed if debt levels and debt service costs are already high. Indeed, the higher the debt levels, the less space there is to apply a structural balance rule because it might be too expensive or there may be no credit to finance the acyclicality of expenditures during downturns. Given that structural balance rules become less acyclical when debt levels are high, the differences in welfare gains between structural balance rules and budget balance rules tend to narrow.

Moreover, adopting structural balance rules may be infeasible for governments with limited access to credit markets. Financial risks increase during economic downturns if the interest rate on debt increases as government debt increases (that is, if there is a debt-elastic interest rate spread). If the sensitivity of interest rate spreads to debt increases, it may not be possible to postpone fiscal consolidation to smooth even a temporary commodity price shock, as accumulating

FIGURE 3.7: **Spillovers from Oil Prices to Nonresource GDP in Algeria, Trinidad and Tobago, 1960–2015**

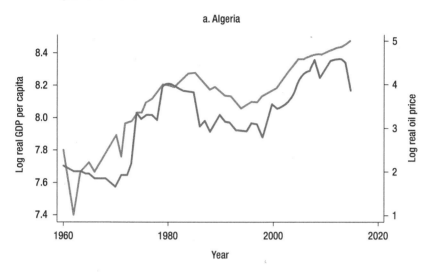

a. Algeria

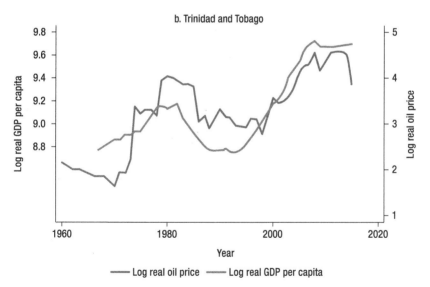

b. Trinidad and Tobago

—— Log real oil price   —— Log real GDP per capita

Source: Pennings and Mendes 2017.

government debt would cause a rapid rise in interest rates, intensifying default risks. In this scenario, the government could avoid adverse changes in its net asset position by adopting a more procyclical fiscal stance than a structural balance rule would allow.

Summary of Findings

Fiscal rules can strengthen macrofiscal policies in smaller economies. For smaller countries that experience significant GDP volatility and tend to have procyclical, deficit-biased fiscal policies, implementing a fiscal rule can signal a strong commitment to fiscal prudence, with positive implications for debt sustainability, output stabilization, and consumption among vulnerable households unable to smooth fluctuations in their income. More generally, fiscal rules can make fiscal policy more predictable and credible, allowing governments to adopt an acyclical or countercyclical stance without generating unsustainable debt concerns and reducing borrowing costs.

Policy makers must weigh the relative advantages and drawbacks of various fiscal rules and select those that best reflect their economic circumstances and policy priorities. The characteristics of each country's business cycle should inform the selection of the most effective fiscal rule. Countries with asymmetric business cycles require higher savings rates during shorter expansions to finance larger deficits during longer recessions, which may be politically difficult to achieve and require substantial policy credibility. Debt rules and budget balance rules establish a clear, direct link with debt sustainability, but they tend to exacerbate the amplitude of the business cycle. Structural balance rules contribute to stabilizing output and strengthening social insurance. Their link with debt sustainability depends on the characteristics of the economy, initial debt conditions, and the commodity price cycle. Expenditure rules can make spending acyclical, so they may replicate the functioning of structural balance rules but are not linked directly to debt sustainability. However, they can trigger the fiscal consolidation necessary to maintain debt sustainability when accompanied by a debt rule or a budget balance rule.

Given their ability to stabilize the business cycle, smooth household consumption, and strengthen the social insurance effects of fiscal policy, structural balance rules appear to be the optimal fiscal rule for smaller countries facing significant macroeconomic volatility. The larger welfare effects of structural balance rules reflect their ability to reduce the procyclicality of public spending, and, given the pervasive procyclicality observed among smaller countries, fiscal rules that promote acyclicality tend to yield substantial welfare gains. The major advantage of structural balance rules is that they shield expenditures from temporary fluctuations in revenue. As many smaller countries face highly procyclical fiscal policies, the welfare gains of structural balance rules can be substantial. By contrast, debt rules and budget balance rules have a much more modest effect in reducing high procyclicality.

However, structural balance rules can be less advantageous in smaller economies in some cases. These include situations where (a) shocks are persistent (more permanent than temporary), (b) changes in commodity prices have a large spillover effect on nonresource GDP, or (c) initial debt levels are high or governments face credit constraints.

Moreover, implementing, monitoring, and maintaining structural balance rules present technical and institutional difficulties that may render them less practical for many smaller economies. While structural balance rules can be highly effective, they are more complex and less transparent than other types of fiscal rules. Technical difficulties and errors (evidenced ex post) are common in the calculations of specific variables needed to estimate structural balance rules, particularly in low- and middle-income economies that are converging and have significant GDP volatility. Changes and adjustments can erode public and market credibility, which is central to sustaining these mechanisms over time. Successfully implementing a structural balance rule requires great public scrutiny, a robust political consensus, detailed data availability, and sophisticated technical expertise.

The adoption of a combination of debt rules with expenditure rules or of debt rules with budget balance rules can mimic the effects of structural balance rules and ensure debt sustainability, with more simplicity and transparency. Combining expenditure rules with debt rules, for example, can favor debt sustainability while reducing the procyclicality of government spending. The findings of this study indicate that debt rules are easier to implement and to comply with. And implementing an expenditure rule can reduce expenditure procyclicality by as much as 40 percent, helping to address the shortcomings of the debt rule, which has no impact on the accumulation of debt growth below the ceiling. This report shows that these combinations have a positive effect on compliance and performance. These rules are easier for stakeholders to understand and simpler to implement, gaining credibility and support for their establishment and sustainability over time.

Furthermore, combinations of these rules can also be supported by well-defined escape clauses and sovereign wealth funds. The inclusion of well-defined escape clauses can enhance the effectiveness of fiscal rules by increasing their flexibility to address uncommon shocks without undermining their credibility. An escape clause could be triggered by a sharp drop in GDP or by a specific idiosyncratic shock such as a natural disaster.[8] Without an escape clause, the expenditure reduction necessary to satisfy the budget balance rule or debt rule, for example, could potentially exacerbate a shock or deepen an economic downturn. Sovereign wealth funds that are fully integrated with the government budget and are interacting with fiscal rules can reduce revenue volatility, which is one of the factors that exacerbates expenditure volatility and procyclicality. If a sovereign wealth fund is used, a strong link between the fund's accumulation and use mechanisms and a fiscal rule is critical. This link would help to smooth the high volatility faced by smaller economies while maintaining fiscal sustainability.

Notes

This chapter is based on two background papers prepared for this study: Pennings and Mendes (2017) and Aguirre (2017).

1. Wren-Lewis (2011) presents a comprehensive list of the causes of deficit bias. Wyplosz (2013) highlights two causes as especially important: (a) policy makers' incentive to foist the burden of discipline onto future administrations and (b) the interplay of democratic processes and interest group politics. Both phenomena reflect the so-called "common pool" problem, which describes the tendency of those that benefit from higher public spending or lower taxes to ignore the costs they impose on other taxpayers, either contemporaneously or in the future (see Debrun and Kumar 2007).

2. Depending on the purposes they serve, sovereign wealth funds can be classified as (a) *stabilization funds*, where the objective is to insulate the budget and the economy against commodity price swings and the effects of the economic cycle; or (b) *savings funds*, where the objective is to convert nonrenewable assets into a more diversified portfolio of assets to be used by future generations or to ensure funds for long-term liabilities. See Ossowski et al. (2008) and Villafuerte (2015).

3. In this model, agents are assumed to be heterogeneous and to differ by their wealth, income, and employment status, which in turn are related to their education levels. Agents may be employed or unemployed for short or extended periods. Aggregate fluctuations are especially costly for households that are that are more vulnerable to unemployment. Government spending finances public goods and services as well as transfer payments to households. These transfers play a social insurance role, as they attenuate the effects of aggregate economic fluctuations.

4. Budget balance rules with numerical target values equal to 0 impose the condition that spending should be equal to revenue in any period. More generally, these rules enable spending to be different from revenue by the size and sign of the numerical target value, enabling deficits or surpluses.

5. Revenue volatility in very small countries is 3.2 percent of GDP compared to 2.1 percent in large countries.

6. Asymmetric cycles occur when GDP falls by more than 2 standard deviations. These shocks have a 2 percent annual probability of occurring in small countries, and they typically last for eight quarters. When GDP falls by more than 2 standard deviations, the unemployment rate increases by 2 standard deviations.

7. The model assumes two types of households: (a) those that have access to credit markets and can smooth income shocks and (b) those that are financially constrained and consume their total income in each period, which creates an incentive for government to smooth commodity prices and other shocks. Fiscal rules determine how public transfers to households respond to changes in commodity prices (assuming that the government receives all commodity revenues) as well as to changes in nonresource GDP and the government's asset position.

8. For example, an escape clause could allow a budget balance rule's deficit limit to rise from 1 percent of GDP to 2 percent if the GDP growth rate slows to 1 percent or lower during two consecutive quarters and to 3 percent if the growth rate turns negative for two consecutive quarters. The budget balance rule's deficit limit also could be increased by the size of the cost of addressing the effects of a natural disaster, up to the equivalent of 1 percent of GDP. The escape clause could allow for a deviation of up three years in the case of a deceleration of GDP, with at least a minimum reduction of the increase of one-third per year or a return to the budget balance rule limit once the rate of growth of GDP exceeds 1 percent for four consecutive quarters.

References

Aguirre, Alvaro. 2017. "Welfare Effects of Fiscal Rules with Heterogeneous Agents in Small Open Economies." Background paper, World Bank, Washington, DC. http://documents.worldbank .org/curated/en/299961597691885453/Welfare-Effects-of-Fiscal-Rules-with-Heterogeneous -Agents-in-Small-Open-Economies.

Aguirre, Alvaro. 2018. "Welfare Effects of Fiscal Procyclicality: Public Insurance with Heterogeneous Agents." Working Paper 863, Central Bank of Chile, Santiago.

Debrun, Xavier, and Manmohan S. Kumar. 2007. "The Discipline-Enhancing Role of Fiscal Institutions: Theory and Empirical Evidence." IMF Working Paper 07/171, International Monetary Fund, Washington, DC.

Engel, Eduardo, Christopher Nielson, and Rodrigo Valdés. 2013. "Chile's Fiscal Rule as Social Insurance." In *Fiscal Policy and Macroeconomic Performance*, 393–425. Santiago: Central Bank of Chile.

González, Gustavo, Francisco Muñoz, and Klaus Schmidt-Hebbel. 2013. "Optimal Dynamic Fiscal Policy with Applications to Chile and Norway." Working Paper, Pontifical Catholic University of Chile.

Kumhof, Michael, and Douglas Laxton. 2013. "Simple Fiscal Rules for Small Open Economies." *Journal of International Economics* 91 (1): 113–27.

Medina, Juan Pablo, and Claudio Soto. 2016. "Commodity Prices and Fiscal Policy in a Commodity Exporting Economy." *Economic Modelling* 59 (December): 335–51.

Ossowski, Rolando Mauricio Villafuerte, Paulo Medas, and Theo Thomas. 2008. "Managing the Oil Revenue Boom: The Role of Fiscal Institutions." IMF Occasional Paper 260, International Monetary Fund, Washington, DC.

Pennings, Steven, and Arthur Mendes. 2017. "Consumption Smoothing and Shock Persistence: Optimal Simple Rules for Commodity Exporters." Policy Research Working Paper 8035, World Bank, Washington, DC. http://documents.worldbank.org/curated/en/384311493124785251 /pdf/WPS8035.pdf.

Pieschacón, Anamaría 2012. "The Value of Fiscal Discipline for Oil-Exporting Countries." *Journal of Monetary Economics* 59 (3): 250–68.

Schaechter, Andrea, Tidiane Kinda, Nina Budina, and Anke Weber. 2012. "Fiscal Rules in Response to the Crisis: Toward the 'Next-Generation' Rules—a New Dataset." IMF Working Paper 12/187, International Monetary Fund, Washington, DC.

Villafuerte, Mauricio. 2015. "Fiscal Policy Management and Sovereign Wealth Funds." In *Sovereign Funds: Fiscal Framework, Governance, and Investment,* edited by Ana María Jul and Donghyun Park. London: Central Banking Publications.

Wren-Lewis, Simon. 2011. "Comparing the Delegation of Monetary and Fiscal Policy." Discussion Paper 540, Department of Economics, Oxford University, Oxford.

Wyplosz, Charles. 2013. "Fiscal Rules: Theoretical Issues and Historical Experiences." In *Fiscal Policy after the Crisis,* edited by Alberto Alesina and Franceso Giavazzi, 496–525. Chicago: University of Chicago Press.

4

Summing Up: Implementing Practical Fiscal Rules in Smaller Countries

Due to their greater openness, low economic diversification, and exposure to natural disasters, smaller countries tend to face higher macroeconomic volatility. Indeed, throughout the 2000s, small countries exhibited lower and more volatile growth of GDP than larger countries. Smaller countries tend to experience shorter expansions and deeper recessions; they are especially prone to terms-of-trade shocks; and they are more likely to suffer from fiscal instability and unsustainable debt dynamics. All of these trends are more acute in smaller and very small LAC countries.

High indebtedness, spending procyclicality, and, in many cases, a series of natural disasters have exacerbated macroeconomic volatility and hampered GDP growth in small LAC countries. The strong volatility of international markets and the impact of the 2008 global financial crisis disproportionately affected small economies, as government deficits and debt undermined macroeconomic stability and lowered GDP growth rates. This pattern was especially pronounced in small LAC countries. Economic growth among small and very small economies was 20 and 34 percent lower, respectively, than growth among large countries in the region. In addition, the negative impacts of recurrent natural disasters in small and very small LAC countries—in particular, the Caribbean countries—resulted in heightened volatility, significant GDP slowdown, and accelerated indebtedness associated with high fiscal costs to repair damaged infrastructure.

In smaller countries, fiscal policy plays an even more critical role in ensuring resilience to economic shocks, reducing volatility, and preserving fiscal sustainability. Governments tend to be larger, and the impact of fiscal policy on aggregate demand tends to be stronger in smaller countries than in larger economies. In addition, due to the more extensive use of less flexible exchange rate regimes, the stabilizing role of fiscal policy becomes even more critical for smaller economies. It can exert a central role in saving resources in good times to be used in downturns and thus helps to stabilize their more frequent and deeper fluctuations in output.

Fiscal policy mechanisms can help reduce volatility. In this context, fiscal rules may be an attractive policy option for smaller countries in LAC. Adopting and adhering to fiscal rules signal a strong commitment to debt sustainability and help to reduce output volatility, with positive implications for smoothing employment and consumption among vulnerable groups of the population. Rules-based fiscal policy can also enhance budgetary credibility and predictability, facilitating access to credit markets facing adverse shocks.

Fiscal rules may also be a critical part of a broader risk management framework in smaller countries, which often face heightened volatility and uncertainty. Aimed at mitigating the impact of adverse exogenous shocks, risk management strategies combine insurance or risk transfer tools with precautionary or self-insurance mechanisms. In coping with disasters and other environmental hazards that negatively affect GDP growth, the most vulnerable groups of the population, and the government's financial position, many governments have contracted for weather-related insurance to transfer the risk of events with highly negative impact. Precautionary or self-insurance instruments consist of building buffers such as sovereign funds or access to contingent credit instruments for the purpose of offsetting a fall in revenue or unexpected costs generated by adverse shocks. In this regard, some type of fiscal rule that enables authorities to save fiscal resources in good times so they can spend them in rainy periods can be considered a precautionary or self-insurance mechanism, enhancing the efficiency of a country's risk management framework.

Given their ability to stabilize the business cycle and smooth household consumption, structural balance rules appear to be well suited for countries facing strong macroeconomic volatility. They require budgetary surpluses while the economy is in an upturn period, helping to reduce the need for large adjustments during downturns and thus preventing procyclical fiscal policy. Indeed, the large welfare effects of structural balance rules reflect their ability to reduce the procyclicality of public spending. Due to the pervasive procyclicality observed in smaller countries, fiscal rules that promote acyclicality may yield substantial welfare gains.

Nonetheless, structural balance rules may be far less advantageous in cases where (a) economic shocks are persistent, (b) changes in commodity prices have a large spillover effect on nonresource GDP, (c) debt levels are high, or (d) the government's ability to borrow is limited—all of which can be common in smaller economies. Using a structural balance rule to smooth persistent shocks can be counterproductive and may be unsustainable in some situations. If negative commodity price shocks persist, such a rule will postpone adjustments of consumption for financially constrained agents and delay fiscal consolidation, which may cause debt dynamics to become unsustainable, as the government sells assets or accumulates debt to finance a budgetary shortfall that, for practical purposes, may be permanent.

Initial debt conditions also should guide the selection of rules because, in contexts of high indebtedness, the objectives of fiscal sustainability and output stabilization are not necessarily compatible, and the first objective should be predominant. High debt levels make output smoothing more difficult and costly. Indeed, the welfare gains from moving to a structural balance rule decrease with debt levels, as higher debt reduces the fiscal space available for smoothing shocks and downturns. A negative output shock increases debt-to-GDP ratios, and a lower increase or even a decrease in spending may be needed if both debt levels and the costs of debt service are already high. The higher the debt levels, the less space is available to apply a structural balance rule.

The design of fiscal rules should be commensurate with the technical and institutional capacities observed in a country. Indeed, institutional and technical capacities and the overall fiscal policy framework are key aspects affecting compliance with and the effectiveness of fiscal rules. The design and implementation of fiscal rules demand different levels of technical capacity. Appropriate GDP projections, proper identification of business cycles, and sound medium-term fiscal frameworks are critical technical aspects underpinning the design of fiscal rules and the definition of their target levels. Strong enforcement mechanisms—including the presence of independent fiscal councils for monitoring compliance with the rule; sound budgetary and public financial management institutional arrangements, such as those ensuring the credibility and coverage of the budget; and strong fiscal accounting systems—favor compliance and effectiveness. Often, the link between fiscal rules and sovereign funds (savings or stabilization funds) helps to improve transparency, strengthen the overall framework and facilitate the achievement of the fiscal and economic objectives pursued.

In this regard, simpler rules may be preferred. From an analytical perspective, ideal rules ensure fiscal sustainability and provide flexibility to attenuate fluctuations in output and consumption. From a practical point of view, more effective rules are simple to understand, easy to communicate to all stakeholders (including the general public), and easy to implement. Capacity constraints, complexity, data availability, and transparency issues can hamper implementation, as discussed earlier. Complex structural balance rules that are difficult to communicate and comprehend may, in some cases, erode public and political support, which is central to sustaining fiscal rules over time. Technical constraints regarding the estimation of potential outputs, cycles, and trends that are highly sensitive to GDP revisions, the value of revenue elasticities and expenditure multipliers, and the difficulty of real-time macroeconomic monitoring for assessing compliance can make structural balance rules less practical, especially for smaller economies or for any country with limited data and capacity constraints.

With more simplicity, more transparency, and fewer technical requirements, the combination of expenditure rules with debt rules or expenditure rules with budget balance rules is capable of ensuring debt sustainability and matches the smoothing effects of structural balance rules. Combining expenditure rules with debt rules, for example, can favor debt sustainability simultaneously while reducing the procyclicality of government spending. This approach combines the stabilizing properties of an expenditure rule with the effective debt-controlling properties of a debt or a budget balance rule. Adopting a ceiling on expenditure growth reduces the procyclicality of expenditures, whereas a ceiling on revenues acts as an automatic stabilizer, addressing the shortcoming of the debt rule, which has no impact on the accumulation of debt growth below the ceiling. When debt levels are close to the targeted level, the debt rule is activated and becomes the binding constraint, ensuring that debt will follow a sustainable path and enhancing credibility. Further flexibility can be provided by including escape clauses to be triggered under exceptional circumstances (such as deep recessions or natural disasters) that require a more forceful expenditure reaction than the ceiling on expenditure growth allows.

Empirical results from this study confirm that expenditure rules tend to reduce expenditure procyclicality and that this effect is stronger when combined with a fiscal council and a sovereign wealth fund. This study provides evidence of the positive effect that these combinations have on compliance and performance. These rules are easier to understand and simpler for government to implement, gaining credibility and support for their sustainable compliance over time. Among the global sample of countries, only expenditure rules have a significant impact on reducing fiscal procyclicality. The presence of an enforcement mechanism, such as a fiscal council or a sovereign wealth fund, further enhances the stabilizing effect of expenditure rules. Among smaller countries, the impact of expenditure rules on expenditure procyclicality is more modest, but still significant.

Well-designed, well-implemented fiscal rules are a suitable mechanism for all countries, but they are particularly critical for smaller economies. This study discusses various findings and lessons from both theory and practice that clearly demonstrate the importance of having well-designed fiscal rules that fit macroeconomic, external, and other country characteristics. Moreover, with proper establishment, implementation and compliance, fiscal rules can help to achieve significantly better fiscal outcomes, less procyclical policies, more output smoothing, and, through that, better welfare results for citizens of a country. In addition, design features depend on the country's initial fiscal and debt conditions, institutional settings, and technical capacities. Obtaining the long-term support of key stakeholders and achieving good results depend on a fiscal rule(s) framework designed with simplicity, transparency, and strong accountability mechanisms. This study argues that many of the findings and lessons discussed apply roughly similarly to economies of different sizes. However, there are some differences in impact and effectiveness of fiscal rules between smaller and larger economies. If well designed and well implemented, fiscal rules are good for all countries, but they are essential for smaller economies, given their special characteristics. Indeed, having a fiscal rules mechanism can be an essential policy mechanism in smaller economies. Nonetheless, and despite the evidence, policy makers, stakeholders (local and international), and economic observers have yet to grasp the criticality of this topic for these economies.

ECO-AUDIT
Environmental Benefits Statement

The World Bank Group is committed to reducing its environmental footprint. In support of this commitment, the Publishing and Knowledge Division leverages electronic publishing options and print-on-demand technology, which is located in regional hubs worldwide. Together, these initiatives enable print runs to be lowered and shipping distances decreased, resulting in reduced paper consumption, chemical use, greenhouse gas emissions, and waste.

The Publishing and Knowledge Division follows the recommended standards for paper use set by the Green Press Initiative. The majority of our books are printed on Forest Stewardship Council (FSC)–certified paper, with nearly all containing 50–100 percent recycled content. The recycled fiber in our book paper is either unbleached or bleached using totally chlorine-free (TCF), processed chlorine-free (PCF), or enhanced elemental chlorine-free (EECF) processes.

More information about the Bank's environmental philosophy can be found at http://www.worldbank.org/corporateresponsibility.